"Impressively informative, expertly organized and presented, 'The Book Review Companion' is unreservedly recommended for author, publisher and book publicists professional reference collections. Especially commended for community and academic library Writing/Publishing collections."
— ***Midwest Book Review***

"Book reviews are the lifeblood of many successful book launches. David Wogahn's book cuts through the confusion to show both indie- and traditionally-published authors an effective system for getting the reviews their books deserve. Highly recommended."
— ***Joel Friedlander,*** *TheBookDesigner.com*

"David has written one of the most useful books for book marketing. We all know that book reviews are the single most important aspect of a book's success, yet they are a mystery to most authors. David provides straightforward advice about the many types of reviews and how best to secure them. From timing, to guidelines to strategies, this book has it all. A must read for all authors."
— ***Fauzia Burke,*** *president, FSB Associates and author, Online Marketing for Busy Authors*

"Reviews, in my opinion, are just as important as the cover and title of the book. Readers need to see a solid base of reviews to make a decision to buy your book. *The Book Review Companion* is a comprehensive guide to understanding why reviews matter, and how to get them."
— ***Jim Kukral,*** *Founder, Author Marketing Club*

"Reviews are key to book sales. David Wogahn has created an indispensable roadmap for requesting and garnering reviews in this essential resource for authors."
— *Best-selling mystery author,* **Elizabeth Spann Craig**

"If you are going to advertise your book—something I think every author should do—you don't want to send shoppers to a page with no or few reviews. David Wogahn's book is covers everything about book reviews; Amazon policies, sources, ARCs, even writing reviews to build your platform. It's all there."
—**Dave Chesson,** *Kindle Marketing Jedi, Kindlepreneur.com*

THE BOOK REVIEW
COMPANION

Also by David Wogahn

My Publishing Imprint

Register Your Book, 2nd Edition

The Book Reviewer Yellow Pages, 9th Edition

Successful eBook Publishing

Marketing and Distributing eBooks
(LinkedIn Learning)

THE BOOK REVIEW COMPANION

An Author's Guide to Getting and Using Book Reviews

 DAVID WOGAHN

PartnerPress
Carlsbad, California

The Book Review Companion:
An Author's Guide to Getting and Using Book Reviews
© 2019 David Wogahn, All Rights Reserved.

www.DavidWogahn.com

Available in these formats:
- 978-1-944098-14-8 (Paperback)
- 978-1-944098-15-5 (eBook)

Library of Congress Control Number: 2019948358

Editing: Katie Barry
Cover design: Anton Stefanov Rangelov
Publishing Services: Kerri Esten, AuthorImprints
Audiobook producer: Carter Wogahn

Published by PartnerPress | Carlsbad, California

For volume and resale pricing, please contact publish@partnerpress.org

My favorite writer is Jane Austen,
and I've read all her books
so many times I've lost count.

—J.K. Rowling

· · · · ·

Every time I read 'Pride and Prejudice'
I want to dig her up and beat her over
the skull with her own shin-bone.

—Mark Twain

Contents

The Countdown to Book Launch™ Series

The Countdown to Book Launch series is for authors, self-publishers, and small presses with limited time and a need for authoritative publishing information informed by real-world experience. Each book focuses on its intended topic and avoids fluff or filler material.

The material presented in each book has been thoroughly researched and recommendations are made based on personal experience. But as it can be with how-to guides, information and resource links are subject to change over time. I help readers cope with this in two unique ways.

1. Hyperlinks to online references in each book are replaced with a URL link shortener domain: breve.link. It works like Bitly or TinyURL; long, complicated links are replaced with easy-to-read and maintain links. It allows us to keep the links in your book working and makes it easier to look-up links if you are reading the paperback.

2. Members of my mailing list receive advance notice about exclusive launch offers when I release a book or training resource. Join my mailing list at:

DavidWogahn.com/join

or subscribe to one of the free resources at AuthorImprints.com to be notified.

> To your success,
> David Wogahn
>
> DavidWogahn.com
> AuthorImprints.com

Preface

This book is a direct result of a book review I posted on Amazon in 2016.

The actual story began much earlier, in 2011, when a blurb on Teleread mentioned readers could get a free copy of *The Book Reviewer Yellow Pages*. Always fascinated by directories (I published *Golf Yellow Pages* for six years), I grabbed a copy. It was my introduction to the world of book bloggers and the art and science of soliciting book reviews.

Two years later I bought the fourth edition, in print, and boy was I disappointed. Not only was the layout and design unwieldy, but much of the advice about using the book and getting reviews had been eliminated. I took to Amazon to share my constructive criticism and never thought about it again—until I got a voice mail (yes, a phone call) from the author on a Saturday afternoon during the holidays. Not only did she appreciate the feedback, she wanted me to know that all my points were addressed in the fifth edition and asked if I would like a copy.

I went on to write the foreword for the sixth edition and contributed an article to the seventh edition. Not only that, when the original author, Christine Pinheiro, decided to stop publishing after the eighth edition, she offered me the opportunity to take over as publisher.

By this point I had a far greater appreciation for the importance of reviews, and the nuances of getting and using reviews—both reader reviews and endorsements, or blurbs. In my author services business, AuthorImprints, I was witnessing firsthand the difficulties authors were experiencing getting those critical early reviews.

It didn't seem to matter whether this was their first book, or fifth book, whether they were writing fiction or nonfiction. Traditionally published authors also seem to struggle. In fact, it is sometimes harder for these authors because they can't easily take advantage of tactics available to authors who control their eBook pricing and book sale promotions.

What was clear is that most authors needed a roadmap that detailed timing, tactics, and specific how-to information; a resource they could keep referring back to as they progressed from finishing their manuscript through to the post-release period when sales happen. Seeking book reviews is a never-ending pursuit for any author.

I also observed it was possible to be proactive when it comes to accumulating book reviews. It's a topic and strategy I shared in a guest post for Jane Friedman's blog in early 2018, titled "The Essential First Step for New Authors: Book Reviews, Not Sales." I've since employed it with all our launch marketing clients, and it works every time to generate early and generally more favorable reviews.

The Book Review Companion is just that, a *companion* for an author's *book review journey*. A resource long on tactics and specifics, and short on prose and opinion. I hope you keep it handy and refer to it often.

• • • • •

One thing I did differently for this book was to share early drafts extensively. What good is a field manual that hasn't been field tested? My reviewers—new authors and experienced publishing professionals alike—were especially helpful (and sometimes brutal): Jacki Day, Jan Janice, Steve Baska, Lee Van Ham, Barbara Lacy, Peggy Nehmen, Jim Halverson, Mo Horvath, David Moschella, Lincoln Stoller, Lynette Smith, Jacqueline Holness, Richard Ennis, Mardy Grothe, and Manon Wogahn.

This book is further enriched by the contributions of authors who wished to share their personal stories. Inside you will find advice from Marj Charlier,

Mikel Miller, Jill Thomas, Anna-Marie Abell, and Cherie Kephart.

• • • • •

To think, all this came about because someone gave their book away—for free.

Start Here

Show me an author not thinking about book reviews, and I'll show you an author unprepared to publish, or struggling to ignite sales if their book is already launched. Reviews take on even greater importance for books sold online—where most books are sold today.

My goal for writing *The Book Review Companion* is to give you a resource you can turn to during the different phases of your book marketing journey. There are steps to take and tactics to consider before your book is released. The launch period is another phase that benefits from planning and careful tending to soliciting reviews. And once your book is gathering reviews, the journey doesn't end.

Start Here is a quick reference directory to the most important concepts and resources in *The Book Review Companion*. Chances are, not all the information will be applicable when you first read it. Come back to this chapter when you need new ideas, get stuck, or need a refresher.

Reviews come from three sources: contacts, spending money, or sales

When thinking about book reviews, I find it helps to divide the source of reviews into three groups: contacts, money, and sales. It is also important to pursue reviews in this same order, as explained in Chapter 2, Three Guiding Principles.

Contacts: This group includes everyone from acquaintances to a member of your mailing list or a social media connection. Contacts will be most familiar with your writing and you as author, and the ones most willing to help.

- Chapter 2: Understand why this group is your most important resource.
- Chapter 4: See source 1, your most important source for book reviews.

Money: This is the second way to generate reviews.

- Chapter 3: Make sure you understand Amazon's policies about paying for reviews and buying or giving books to reviewers.
- Chapter 4: Most of the spending for reviews is to pay for editorial reviews and several of the sources in this chapter require a financial investment. See sources 5, 7, 8, and 9.

Sales: You need people reading your book whether they pay full price, get a discount, or receive a free copy. Generally, you have no idea who these people are because you cannot choose them like you can with contacts (to whom you might also give a free copy of your book).

- Chapter 3: Amazon has specific policies for soliciting reviews using free or discounted books.
- Chapter 4: See source 3 (Giveaways/Promos).

Turn to Bonus 2, The New Author Conundrum, for more detail.

There are two types of reviews: customer and editorial

Customer reviews are those left on websites like Amazon along with a star rating. Editorial reviews are complimentary statements about you or your book written by someone that your audience will recognize.

- The differences between these two reviews are described in Chapter 3, as are Amazon's policies regarding soliciting them.
- The ten sources in Chapter 4 are labeled as either ideal for seeking customer reviews or seeking editorial reviews.
- How to use editorial reviews (and blurbs) is covered in detail in Chapter 6. Also in Chapter 6 you'll find an analysis of editorial reviews for three top indie books. The results are surprising

and show that at least these authors didn't pay for editorial reviews for these books yet they are doing just fine.

Proactively seek reviews, in a specific sequence, before sales promotions

One of the most effective uses of time for an author is seeking reviews before their book is published. This is done by the author, their publisher, or a publicist by sending out copies of the book, called ARCs—advance review or reading copies—in print or electronic format, to a select group of people.

- Chapter 2 explains the four groups of potential reviewers you can approach and the order in which to do so.
- Nine of the ten sources in Chapter 4 are acceptable ways to get early reviews. The possible exception is source 3, Giveaways/Promotions, which generally requires a book that has been published.
- Chapter 7 is all about ARCs. What versions of the book to send, how or if you should label your ARCs, and many other details.

Once you have reviews, what do you do with them?

- Editorial reviews can be put to work as soon as your book is available for pre-order, helping you market your book. See Chapter 6.

- Customer reviews, in most cases, cannot be posted until a book is published. The notable exceptions are Goodreads, which allows members to post reviews prior to release date, and anyone who wants to publish a review on their website.

For most of us it's the Amazon customer reviews that count most. Simply ask your reviewers to hold their review until the release date and then post it. See Chapter 3 for specifics about Amazon policies.

Finally, why do I recommend not promoting your book until it has several book reviews? See Chapter 1 and Chapter 2.

Recognize the ten sources of reviews, when to use them, and how to use them in your marketing

- Chapter 4 is divided into ten sources for getting book reviews. Some of these, like sources 1, 2, 6, and 10 do not cost any money. They do take time, some level of expertise, and perhaps luck, but anyone can use them.
- I devote all of Chapter 5 to finding and approaching bloggers.

Navigate Amazon policies, ignore the myths, and take advantage of their resources

Chapter 3 has a complete guide to Amazon policies regarding reviews, including the $50 rule. This chapter also goes into detail about dealing with negative reviews.

Endorsements and blurbs: quoting nice things that other people say about you or your book

Amazon permits authors or their publishers to feature quotes on a book's page. These are called editorial reviews and while they are different from customer reviews (those with stars), they are still important. There are also useful in all sorts of other ways: on your website, in or on your book, and in your marketing materials.

Chapter 6 is where to turn for details about:

- Why they are worth getting
- Asking for blurbs before your book is released
- Editing and formatting rules
- How to use them

The question to keep coming back to when seeking and using blurbs is: Who are you trying to impress?

Advance review copies of books

Generating interest for your book prior to the publication date is one of the most effective marketing investments you can make. Creating sales materials is one way. But the best way to promote a book is to get people reading it.

Also, if you are seeking endorsements and blurbs in advance of publication, those you are approaching will want to see the book.

Not surprisingly, there are different ways to accomplish this. And like any type of intellectual property, especially books in digital format, there are considerations for how you share your hard work—especially since you aren't making any money in this case.

I reference ARCs throughout this book. However, I cover the topic in greater depth in Chapter 7.

1

Why Reviews Matter

"While we may not realize it, we see Social Proof around us all the time . . . When in a retail outlet, we also use Social Proof to decide if it is safe to buy from."

— *Fast Company,*
The Secret Power Behind Why We Pick
Crowded Restaurants Over Empty Ones

The challenge for every new book, and especially for new authors who have small or nonexistent networks of eager fans, is to convince readers to add one more title to their to-be-read pile. Readers are looking for proof—proof that a book is worth their time to read.

Unfortunately, most new authors do not (yet) have a reputation that confers credibility upon their books. That's where book reviews can help; they contribute credibility and raise awareness in four distinct ways:

1. Customer reviews encourage shoppers to learn more. Reader reviews are a social signal, much like a full parking lot or a line in a store is a signal of popularity. The importance of customer reviews has increased as more books are sold online.

Having numerous outstanding customer reviews on a retailer's website acts as a positive social signal to readers, encouraging them to buy the book. Nowhere is this more important than on Amazon.

2. Reviews add gravitas. There are two types of reviews: editorial reviews and customer-written reviews. The customer-written reviews are those with stars that you see on websites like Amazon and Goodreads.

Editorial reviews are written by those presumed to be experts with a book's subject matter or the author's expertise and they play a different role. These are often used on the back cover, placed inside the book, or used in sales materials. These reviews are intended to impress key audiences such as book retailers and librarians, but also the discerning reader.

Positive editorial reviews can help a book get into the hands of these gatekeepers, but authors need to be careful with how they use them. A leading distributor of books published by small presses, Small

Press United, points out that one reason for declining some books is because "Quotes used on the front and/or back covers are not from people with impressive credentials."

In other words, the source for your quote(s) should be credible to the audience you are marketing to, or the review may result in the opposite effect to what is desired.

By the way, sometimes it's not what is said, but who says it. A quote from the right individual or organization could open doors and create opportunities.

3. Reviews are marketing. It is not uncommon for the media to contact authors after seeing a review posted online or finding it in an online search. This very thing happened to *A Few Minor Adjustments* author Cherie Kephart, who told me: "One blogger loved my book so much that I made it to her top 20 books read in 2017. Also, from her promotion of my book I was contacted for a radio interview."

Bloggers are a particularly unique resource to help in this regard. The trick is to find the right ones and to get them excited enough about your book to read it. It can be challenging, but it's worth the effort.

4. Reviews are a signal to third parties. Common book marketing tactics include contacting the media and bloggers to feature you and your book, giving talks to local groups, appearing on podcasts, and scheduling online book promotions. Many people you contact will look at your book's online listing to read what other people are saying before they reply.

Most book promotion websites will have minimum review requirements before considering a book for promotion—both in quantity and average stars. Why? For the first reason stated above: customer reviews encourage shoppers to learn more.

Bottom line: numerous (positive) reviews help your book sell more copies, be seen more favorably, and attract more promotional opportunities.

I know you are eager to skip ahead to learning where to find reviewers, and how to approach them, but first we need to cover the basics. If you are getting ready to release your first book, or it's been some time since the last one, I suggest reading the next three chapters in this order. After that you can bounce around the various chapters depending on your needs.

2

Three Guiding Principles

"When my Facebook advertising book
came out, I knew I could convince a lot
of people to try Facebook ads—but it
would not work for them. I knew the only
way to get happy customers and 5-star
ratings on Amazon was to *dis*qualify
people who didn't fit."
— Perry Marshall,
80/20 Sales and Marketing

The importance of customer reviews has been
steadily increasing, closely tied to the migration
of bookselling from brick-and-mortar stores
to online retailers. Online, these reviews become
a permanent record of customer satisfaction making it not only imperative that books have reviews,
but that the reviews are written by a book's target
audience.

In this way, the shift to online shopping has forced traditionally published books and self-published books to compete for reader reviews.

Think about it, the vast majority of books sold in stores are published by large publishers. Entire tables are devoted to new releases, and store staff is there to share their "reviews" if not push the sale of those books. This isn't the case in online stores where every book is just one click away from a comparable title.

In other aspects of publishing it is impossible, if not dangerous, to make sweeping generalizations about book marketing. But when it comes to book reviews, I've identified three guiding principles that apply to any book, regardless of who publishes it.

1. An ever-growing number of book reviews is the goal; you don't stop seeking them.
2. A book that has reviews is easier to promote than one without reviews or few of them.
3. To the extent it is possible, seek readers who are the most ideal audience for your book.

1. Don't stop seeking reviews

In 2016, Amazon made a major change to its review policies. One of those changes was to use the date a review was posted on Amazon as a factor in scoring a product's "average review" number. Prior to this that number was simply an average of all stars. From Amazon:

> Amazon calculates a product's star ratings using a machine learned model instead of a raw data average. The machine learned model takes into account factors including: the age of a review, helpfulness votes by customers and whether the reviews are from verified purchases.

So more recent reviews, especially if they are positive, can help increase or maintain your book's overall average customer review rating.

Consider the shopper's perspective

Do shoppers care whether a book has recent reviews? It depends on the subject matter. Certain books can be timeless; their information doesn't become less useful over time.

On the other hand, some categories of nonfiction—how-to, travel, and software manuals are good examples—can become less valuable the older they get. That is certainly the case with my first book, *Successful eBook Publishing*, originally released in 2013.

Where I'm going with this is that chasing book reviews is not limited to your launch plan, it should be part of your ongoing marketing efforts. Perhaps you won't emphasize it as much as when you launched your book but continuing to encourage your readers to leave reviews is something every author should do.

2. Accumulate reviews before promoting

You know how good your work is. You created it. You lived with it through the phases of publication gestation: idea, brainstorming, outline, research, writing, and rewriting. You have improved, enhanced, and polished your work to a degree you didn't think possible. You believe it's perfect.

Alas, your opinion is not the most important at this point in your publishing cycle. You need third-party confirmation to attract readers. You need (positive) independent assessment to convince readers to spend money *and* time on your book.

British sociologist John Thompson, an expert in the influence of the media in the formation of modern societies, identifies the resources or capital that are essential for publishing success in his book *Merchants of Culture: The Publishing Business in the Twenty-First Century*. Thompson writes that besides cash, the most important resource is "symbolic capital," which he defines as: "The accumulated prestige and status associated with the publishing house."

Book reviews build symbolic capital

New authors—and certainly self-published authors—have no symbolic capital. They are not (yet) known for producing quality books that seduce readers to the degree that they are willing to part with some of their disposable income, not to mention time. Is it possible to create this symbolic capital? Absolutely yes, and many have.

In today's increasing online world of book shopping, I argue it is book reviews that build symbolic capital. A shopper evaluating a book for purchase when it has no, or few, reviews is like a hungry guest walking into an empty restaurant. *How good can this place be if no one is eating here?*

Even authors with traditional publishers who have symbolic capital "in the bank" must actively solicit book reviews so their books can succeed in our unimaginably crowded retail market.

3. Ask the right people, in the right order

We like to think our book is for "everyone," but it rarely is. In fact, appealing to *everyone* is actually a strategy to avoid, at least at the early stages.

In their research paper "The Paradox of Publicity: How Awards Can Negatively Affect the Evaluation of Quality," authors Balazs Kovacs and Amanda Sharkey found that average review scores for sixty-four award-winning and nominated books over a four-year period actually decreased once a book was promoted to a wider audience after winning an award.

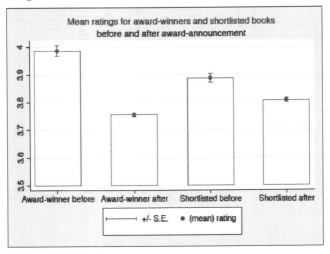

The conclusion? These new readers were not the ideal audience for these books and were reading the book likely out of curiosity. This leads us to finding your ideal readers.

Seek ideal readers first

The key to a successful book launch is prospecting for reviews in safer territories first, then expanding in stages. If you imagine yourself as an explorer in the wilderness of book marketing, your best opportunity for reviews is approaching those familiar with your writing or willing to spend the time reading your book.

The goal is to have some number of reviews in place—the book's social proof and symbolic capital—before investing in general promotions. How many initial reviews should you aim for? Ten is a good initial goal, but have at least five. (One fiction writer told me she doesn't even think about spending money on advertising until she has twenty reviews.)

Let's walk through the four territories illustrated in The Book Review Journey.

The Book Review Journey

The Public

Chosen Reviewers

Addressable Audience

Loyal Fans

AuthorImprints.com

Loyal Fans. These are people who know, like, and trust you. They are also the ones most likely to leave a review. For an established author, they are readers who have reviewed the author's previous books. For new authors, the circle can be small—it depends on the depth of their network and the extent to which that network is familiar with the author's writing.

But be careful—approaching close contacts to review your book carries three risks:

1. Amazon is good at spotting reviews from friends and family and may reject the review (or worse) if it is from a known family member. (For example, someone in your Amazon address book or with whom you share a last name.)
2. If your Loyal Fan network hasn't left reviews for other books, their sole review of your book will carry little weight with shoppers who happen to look at who wrote the review.
3. The third risk relates to number two. Some Loyal Fans go overboard and reference their relationship with the author, or gush without including any meaningful feedback about the book.

Addressable Audience. I define this group as those who have given you permission to contact them, in some way related to your writing or the subject matter of your book. This last part is important. It isn't enough that someone gave you their email address, liked your page/profile, or follows you. If you run a dry-cleaning business and decide to tell your mailing list about your new romance novel, the level of engagement with this list will be proportional to their awareness of you as a romance author.

The purpose of having an Addressable Audience is so you can notify them when you do something they might find interesting, which is presumably the reason why they gave you permission to contact them in the first place.

Addressable Audience members become Loyal Fans when they buy something, and/or act to tell others about it.

Chosen Reviewers. Individuals in the first two groups take time to accumulate and nurture, but this is friendly territory and asking them to review your book should come naturally. Proactively choosing reviewers is different. There are many options and a successful strategy takes time, and potentially money, to execute.

The most important guidance is to seek reviewers who enjoy books like yours. These readers are far more likely to respond favorably to an invitation to invest the time to read your book and offer an informed view.

I call them Chosen Reviewers because you still have some measure of control over whom you approach.

- Book bloggers are a good source of potential reviews. True, they must be willing and available, and even identifying them requires work, but the advantages are: 1) you'll get a review, often posted in multiple places, 2) your book receives promotion when the blogger shares their review on their website and via social media, and 3) there is nearly always no cost to you.

- Blog tour organizers are a second source. They help authors organize review tours—a "virtual book tour" where getting book reviews is the objective (as opposed to promotional tours).
- Reviewers of comparable books. You can make your book available as an advance review copy and submit it to a service like Hidden Gems Books. You can Google comparable books and look for people who have reviewed books similar to yours.

The Public. Unfortunately, this is where many authors begin—the uncharted wilderness. Cold and unforgiving, we're at the mercy of someone who does not know us or does not pay much attention to whether our book is a fit for their reading interests. And that's if they even bother to take a chance since there are few or no reviews. We're living on hope and dying from despair.

The alternative is patience and prioritizing reviews before promotions

The point is that we *do* have control. Instead of a straight-to-the-public Hail Mary, our intrepid explorer has blazed a path through the first three territories of their review journey, *in the order outlined above*. They have several—perhaps ten or more—reviews to show the public before investing in marketing programs to drive readers to their book.

Then when the average shopper arrives, they see social proof; the book has *symbolic capital*.

You cannot control what reviewers say but approaching those most likely to enjoy your book will set the tone for reviews and sales to follow.

What about paid reviews?

I believe that it is too simplistic to say that "spending money on reviews" is a bad idea. There are several perfectly legitimate and ethical instances where spending money is necessary or advantageous.

Rather than make a blanket statement, I say that paying for reviews depends on the book, the author, and the marketing plans for the book, not to mention your budget. Also consider what's important to your primary audience of readers.

Even if you can afford to pay hundreds of dollars for Kirkus to review your book about hiking in Colorado, will readers care? On the other hand, concentrating on Amazon customer reviews is probably just the ticket for your self-published romance book.

Chapter summary

1. Put off advertising your book widely until you have some number of reviews (I suggest five to ten).
2. Start by contacting people familiar with your writing one to three months before the release date.
3. Your goal is to have reviews posted within the first two to three weeks. This way you can run a promotion within the thirty-day new release period. (Amazon favors new releases that people are buying.)
4. Only ask people who have an interest in your type of book to leave a review, to the extent you can control this at the early stage.
5. Don't stop encouraging people to leave reviews.

3

Policies, Ethics, and Rules of the Road

From the *Pirates of the Caribbean*

Elizabeth Turner: "According to the Code..."

Captain Barbossa: "The code is more what you'd call 'guidelines' than actual rules."

Few aspects of book marketing are more frustrating than navigating Amazon's book review policies. Some are specific but everything is open to interpretation—Amazon's interpretation.

Two of the most common misconceptions about proactively seeking book reviews is that doing so is unethical or against Amazon's Terms of Service. Neither is true. As you'll see in Chapter 4, there are lots of established companies that accept payment for writing a book review and Amazon provides a way for those reviews to be posted on book pages.

Let's set the record straight by looking at the facts and the practices that might get a review deleted, or worse, get you or your book banned from the store.

The key point to keep in mind is that you cannot require someone to write a review or require a specific rating such as "five stars" in return for receiving a free or discounted copy of your book.

So, "I'll give you a copy of my book if you'll write a kind review" becomes: "Here is a copy of my book. I'd appreciate it if you would write an honest review."

Never solicit or demand a conditional arrangement, and never hire a company to review your book on the condition that they provide a favorable review. Fortunately, reputable companies don't make guarantees.

Seek arms-length arrangements

The greater the distance between you and the reviewer, the greater the chance the review will be viewed as legitimate.

Here are three examples to illustrate this.

1. Your local writing group, or your buddies in a Facebook group, agree to swap books for the purpose of writing reviews. You all agree to be honest when writing your reviews.

The problem with this arrangement is you all know one another. Putting aside the argument that you promise objectivity when writing a review, it is an easy thing for a company like Amazon to cross-reference review writers to discover they have some type of connection to another author. It has been done, and those reviews are removed.

I had a client who—unbeknownst to me—bought my book and wrote a review. We had no social media connections but somehow Amazon discovered we had a business relationship and the review was removed within a month of its posting.

2. After writing your book, you do an email blast to your mailing list and you offer your book for free with the understanding that those who get it will write a review.

This is much better than the first example. An author's email mailing list is generally made up of fans of the author. Author mailing lists are one of the best marketing tools an author can invest in.

3. You buy a Goodreads Giveaway to give away one hundred copies of your Kindle eBook. Goodreads randomly selects the winners and delivers the eBooks. You do not know who received your book and you have no way to contact them.

These types of arrangements are ideal. A review posted by this reader is completely voluntary. I go into this style of arrangement in more detail in Chapter 4, source 3.

Amazon's book review policies

In 2016, Amazon cracked down on fee-for-review services. The targets were companies that helped product manufacturers and wholesalers get product reviews and those companies went out of business overnight. When announced, it created quite a stir but their exclusion of books from the new policy got muddled in the message. As Amazon's announcement pointed out:

> [These] changes will apply to product categories other than books. We will continue to allow the age-old practice of providing advance review copies of books.

Let's start by defining the difference between Customer Reviews and Editorial Reviews and debunking two myths.

Customer Reviews. These are written by readers who also assign one to five stars to reflect their opinion of the book with five being outstanding. Authors are referring to Customer Reviews when they reference a book's review count on Amazon.

Editorial Reviews. According to Amazon,

. . .an editorial review is a more formal evaluation of a book usually written by an editor or expert within a genre, but can also be written by family and friends.

Myth 1: You cannot pay someone to write a review.

False. Amazon permits payment for editorial reviews.

Myth 2: You cannot give people your book and ask them to review it.

False. You can if you are clear that you welcome all feedback, both positive and negative.

Before Amazon, and before the internet, publishers would haul thousands of ARCs of their forthcoming books to industry tradeshows. These would sit in piles, free for the taking, with no requirements that someone write a review, much less provide their contact information in return for receiving a free copy of the book.

Accomplishing that now is still possible, assuming you stay within Amazon's guidelines.

(See Chapter 6 for instructions about using editorial reviews on Amazon.)

The $50 spending requirement

In 2017 Amazon inserted a new requirement into their Community Guidelines under the heading Eligibility:

> To contribute to Customer features (for example, Customer Reviews, Customer Answers, Idea Lists) or to follow other contributors, you must have spent at least $50 on Amazon.com using a valid credit or debit card in the past 12 months. Promotional discounts don't qualify towards the $50 minimum.

Some have complained that this is overreach and another way for Amazon to force people to buy from them. I don't see it this way. In fact, I consider it a positive.

As a shopper I rely on customer reviews to guide my consideration of a product. How can I make an informed choice if those reviews are polluted by paid reviewers who never bought the product?

That's what was going on. Anyone could write a review and, in fact, reviews were being posted by fake accounts.

Here's an in-depth look at what's permitted, what can get reviews removed, and how reviewers should disclose their relationship to the author.

What's permitted

Direct from Amazon: "You may provide free or discounted copies of your books to readers. However, you may not demand a review in exchange or attempt to influence the review. Offering anything other than a free or discounted copy of the book—including gift cards—will invalidate a review, and we'll have to remove it."

1. Reviewers can remove or edit a review after it is posted.
2. Amazon says that reviews written by friends or a social media connection won't necessarily result in a review being taken down.
3. A reviewer can link to another product—such as their own—if it is relevant and available on Amazon.

When reviews are removed—or worse

- Never invite (or allow) a family member to review your book. Amazon is likely to catch these (as happened to me) before they are posted and will send a nasty email warning.
- I also would not encourage people named in your book to write a review. For example, a foreword writer, your editor, and people named in your acknowledgements.
- If a reader says they wrote a review, but the review was taken down or they say it was never

posted, tell them to contact Amazon by sending an email to community-help@amazon.com.

- Be forewarned that Amazon is both judge and jury regarding what reviews get posted or removed. It is rare for an appeal to succeed.

Penalized with no recourse

Someone with the last name of "Miller" reviewed a colleague's book. The problem is that my colleague's pen name has a surname of "Miller." Amazon killed the review because it appeared this person might be related to him.

What's frustrating about this is: 1) Miller is not his last name and 2) Miller is the sixth most common surname in the U.S., which means that about 18 percent of the U.S. population isn't eligible to review his books.

When you can get a review taken down or modified

If you feel someone's review of your book violates Amazon guidelines or is irrelevant to your book, you can click the "Report abuse" link or email community-help@amazon.com.

Examples of abuses include use of obscenities, a privacy violation, impersonating others, threats, and the usual no-no's: libelous, defamatory, harassing, threatening, or inflammatory statements.

The first review for one of my client's books was written by a disgruntled former employee of his company. In her review she made disparaging remarks about him and the company—clearly not a book review. I reported this to Amazon and the review was removed within a week.

There are also instances where your book is mistaken for another product. I found this four-star review for a book and it obviously is reviewing the wrong product: "I am a large women [sic] and if it hadn't been for the elastic side straps, I think they might not have worked . . . but the[y] did and I am pleased with the quality . . . Just what I wanted!"

Why or how it happens is anyone's guess, but I suggest notifying Amazon.

But also note that if someone makes a negative comment about your book, and you fix what they commented on, they (or Amazon) are not required to change their review to reflect your correction. You can certainly ask them to but changing it is up to them.

Other online stores have similar policies. A while back I noticed a client's recently posted cookbook had a one-star review on Barnes & Noble's website which read:

"It looks stupid. A teen ager told me wat to say."

She contacted the store and they promptly deleted it. It never hurts to ask.

Instruct your reviewers to disclose your relationship

There are many ways for your reviewer to disclose their relationship with you; it just must be conspicuous. They can put it at the end of the review (most often), the beginning, or in the subject line like this first example.

Here is some sample phrasing to use or modify when asking others to write a review for your book. You can also use these in the book reviews you write (you do write reviews, right? See Chapter 9.).

1. In the subject line: *I received an ARC for an objective review.*
2. *I received a copy of this book via* [name of source, such as NetGalley, Edelweiss, the publisher, author] *and I'm reviewing it voluntarily.*
3. *I wrote this review based on an advance review copy that the publisher sent me.*
4. *This review was based on a complimentary pre-release copy.*

Knowing that someone reading an "author-encouraged review" might discount its value, some people will add an additional comment (if true), such as:

- *I've since bought 2 more, one Kindle version for myself and a paperback for . . .*
- *That said, I liked it so much that I bought . . .*

I like to acknowledge my relationship at the end of the review. If I write a review of an advance review copy—and it is rare—it is an honest review that I hope helps the reader decide whether the book is right for them. If you put the disclosure at the top of the review, your review might not get read. If you put it at the end, the reader can decide for herself.

Amazon resources for more details and help

Note: You might need to be logged in or have an account to see some of these pages.

1. **Community guidelines**. Find them here: http://breve.link/brc1

2. The Kindle publishing platform KDP has a good resource in their help section. Login to KDP, in the top menu click **Help**. On the left, click **Promote Your Book**, then click **Customer Reviews**. There you will find several FAQs and answers, which I summarized above.

3. Amazon has a whole section devoted to **Promotional Content** and its relationship to reviews; it's found here: http://breve.link/brc2

4. There are many ways to sell books on Amazon, including SellerCentral (for used and new books). Their policy is found here: http://breve.link/brc3

5. Email Amazon to report problems or issues with reviews: community-help@amazon.com.

Warning: a cautionary tale

I often tell authors that it is important to reciprocate when it comes to book reviews. That is,
reviewing books by other authors. However, you
need to be careful about which books you review
and take steps to avoid any perception that you
might be compromised by a relationship.

Read what my colleague Mikel shares about his
Amazon book review experience:

> Unfortunately, Amazon is often totally
> unresponsive to questions about why they
> removed [my] reviews. I've posted reviews since
> 2009, more than 100 of them, and about three
> months ago Amazon deleted EVERY SINGLE
> ONE of them.
>
> They will not tell me why, except to refer me
> to the guidelines. Yeah, many of the reviews I
> posted were for advance review copies authors
> gave me to review, but many were verified
> Kindle purchases. All of the reviews were
> honest, very few of them 5-stars, and I always
> included a sentence saying I received a copy of
> the book without obligation to post a review.
> Now, Amazon will not let me post any new
> reviews. Go figure.

With no special insight how to avoid Mikel's fate,
my advice is to be selective when reviewing books
written by people you know. You might also go out
of your way to review books by authors you have

no possible way of knowing, living or no longer with us.

Goodreads policies

Goodreads, also owned by Amazon, is even more popular than Amazon as a destination for reviewers who like to post reader reviews. Unlike Amazon, your book does not have to be available for purchase for a reviewer to leave a review.

Goodreads is first and foremost a destination for readers—passionate readers. This is where one can share what they are reading, what they want to read, and what they have read. Goodreads members are much more easily reachable than they would be on Amazon—and this is where it gets sticky.

It is tempting for an author to contact readers of comparable books about reviewing their book. But as soon as you click the button to message that reviewer you will see this Goodreads warning message:

> Note to authors: We don't recommend contacting users to promote your book or request reviews. Nearly all of our members consider unsolicited messages from authors or their representatives to be spam, and sending such messages may result in your account being flagged.

The best way to use Goodreads is as a reader yourself. Become active in the community and in time readers will get to know you. For more about getting involved in this important community of readers, read their author guidelines: http://breve.link/brc4

Negative reviews: to respond or not to respond?

The general rule for responding to a negative reader review is: Don't reply! But if you must, tread lightly.

Treat reviews as market research. If there is a recurring reference to an issue, consider addressing it by updating your book. Poor editing? That's easy to fix. If readers are disappointed you did not cover a topic in a certain way, you can address it in the description so they know about it ahead of time.

Always be honest with the reader and never try to manipulate them into buying your book. This short-term thinking hurts you in the long run.

We also must trust our shoppers that they are smart enough to discount some of these reviews.

I used to publish a golf directory that included U.S. and Canadian golf courses. It was becoming expensive to ensure the Canadian listings were accurate, yet I sold few books in Canada. I eliminated the Canadian courses and changed the title to *U.S.*

Golf Course Directory and promptly got this negative two-star review:

"No Listing of Canadian Courses!! Many excellent courses are available close to US/Canada Border. In Past I believe these were listed."

A board book by one of my clients—one of those thick paged books for babies—was sold in *used condition* by a private party. It too had a negative review that was not the fault of the publisher: the reviewer complained that the book had teeth marks from a toddler.

Sometimes you have to trust that other shoppers will read reviews like these and think more poorly of the reviewer, than your book.

 Keep in mind that your responses are public and your comments and tone will be judged by other shoppers. For an extreme example of how badly things can turn out, read this Buzzfeed article, Who's Afraid of Kathleen Hale? http://breve.link/brc5

Sometimes other reviewers will help

You never want to appear desperate or defensive so it's always more powerful if someone else helps. Fortunately, reviewers will sometimes step in on behalf of authors and come to your defense.

April Hamilton's 2008 edition of *The IndieAuthor Guide* had fifty-one reviews, 90 percent of them five- and four-stars, and a single one-star review. April took issue with the review and posted a compelling response. Other reviewers chimed in mostly in defense of the book. Read it here: http://breve.link/brc6

Stephen Prosapio's *Dream War* received negative comments from a reviewer who accused the author of ripping off the movie *Inception*. In this case the reviewer was mistaken because Stephen's book came out well before *Inception*. A subsequent reviewer (me) corrected him with a follow up review.

Sometimes a lower rating can actually be more helpful

In my LinkedIn group, Marketing on Amazon, a member shared that an author (Pete Morin, *Diary of a Small Fish*) asked him to change his review rating from five-stars to three-stars so that more people would read it. The author liked the review ("Deeply and basically flawed, but a really good read.") and felt that with 93 percent of the reviews either five- or four-stars, few shoppers would discover it. After the reviewer reduced his rating to three-stars the author shared that it actually resulted in a sale.

It's an interesting, and gutsy, marketing strategy. Just keep in mind that everyone has an opinion, as odd as it may seem. I suggest your default position is to let the reader of the review decide for him or herself whether or not to pay attention to the review. As the old saying goes, you can't please everyone.

Chapter summary

1. Never make the gift of your book conditional on getting a review, or worse, asking for special treatment such as a positive review.
2. If you give people a copy of your book, make sure they know they should acknowledge your gift.
3. Reviews written by readers who do not spend at least $50 per year on Amazon will not be posted.
4. Be careful if you plan to ask family or close friends to review your book. Know that their review might not get posted.
5. Do not respond to negative reviews.
6. Take time to understand Amazon's policies and don't hesitate to contact them if you feel a review violates their terms and conditions.

4

Sources of Reviews

"I tell you, if what you have in mind is fame and fortune, publication is going to drive you crazy. If you are lucky, you will get a few reviews, some good, some bad, some indifferent."
— Anne Lamott,
Bird by Bird

There are two ways to get book reviews. You either proactively seek them or passively wait for them to happen. This chapter covers the resources available to those who want to proactively seek reviews—the only way an author can hope to improve their odds of getting "some good" reviews.

There are many sources and methods for seeking book reviews. Each has its own set of benefits, constraints, and applicability to a given book. What works for an experienced, multi-book author probably won't be as effective for a debut author.

Fiction vs. nonfiction books is also a consideration and following the advice of another author is just a starting point. Your tactics will change based on your skills, budget, available time, contacts, and type of book/genre.

But perhaps most importantly for this chapter, there is the critical distinction between the two types of reviews: editorial and customer. If the purpose of a review is to impress and influence someone, who is the person you are trying to impress?

- A shopper?
- A book store manager?
- A librarian?
- A reporter or blogger?
- Some other influencer?

Customer reviews are reviews left by readers who buy, borrow, or are given a book. Many of us call these Amazon reviews but customer reviews can be left in any number of places besides Amazon, for example:

- The reviewer's website
- Goodreads
- LibraryThing
- NetGalley
- Barnes & Noble
- Kobo Books
- Apple Books

Many of these review hubs focus on helping readers find something to read or are online retailers. Readers are free to leave their opinion about a book if they adhere to the website's terms of service.

Thinking about your own book, where do these people who you are trying to impress spend their time? Where do they shop? What do they read? Who impresses them?

Clarity about who you are trying to impress is your compass for navigating possible review sources. Each review source has two facets: the person or organization who wrote the review, and the review itself.

For example, a reader of romance novels is more likely to be influenced by customer reviews on Amazon than they are by a *Kirkus Review*. On the other hand, a children's illustrated book author would love to have a review in *School Library Journal*.

Know who you are trying to impress and where these people turn to discover new books.

Ten review sources

This chapter provides an overview of ten sources for soliciting reviews.

1. Your contacts (which usually includes readers if you are an established author)
2. Book reviewers

3. Giveaways/Promotions
4. Traditional media
5. Review tours
6. Review businesses-traditional
7. Review businesses-fee based
8. Review businesses-hybrid
9. Review businesses-services
10. Book bloggers and websites with blogs

Each source leads off with the primary review goal of either customer reviews or editorial reviews. I then go into detail about the source and conclude with a summary recap that addresses these six criteria for each source.

1. **Your time investment**. How much of your time will this take?
2. **Money or cost**. How much will it cost or what influences the cost?
3. **Experience required**. Do you need special training or skills?
4. **The ability to target ideal readers of your book**. Since this is one of the three guiding principles (See Chapter 2), is this possible? Or how easy is it to do?
5. **Amazon customer reviews**. Some review sources are better suited to securing Amazon customer reviews than others.
6. **Other benefits**. Many of these sources have side benefits more generally known as marketing. In

addition to the review, or in the event you don't get the review you were expecting, are there consolation prizes? The answer for many is yes!

We begin with source 1, your contacts.

Source 1: Your contacts (including your mailing list)

Primary review goal: customer reviews

There is no better investment of your time as an author than creating and nurturing a mailing list. With it, you can solicit beta readers, solicit reviews, and sell books. If approached ethically, the only people on your list are those who want to be there.

I love this quote by Brian Clarke, founder of Copyblogger:

> I have 185,000 Twitter followers. A tweet of content will get me around 20 clicks. Twenty bucks on a boosted Facebook post of the same content to 5,165 people who like the page gets even less. But a link in my newsletter? More than 2,000 clicks from an email list of less than 7,500.

This is not to say that you cannot find reviewers via your social media network. But the point of Brian's quote is that those connections are just one source, and they are often harder to motivate than those on your mailing list. Use social media to stay connected and to help you grow your mailing list.

Getting started

Everyone begins from scratch. However, we all have contacts, it's just a matter of getting them organized and coming up with a plan to contact people. Before my client Susan Old published her first novel, we got her contacts into a mailing list of just fifty-six people and began sharing updates. Two weeks after her book was released, we had eleven Amazon reviews (and none of those were from family members).

Summary recap

- **Your time investment**: At least initially, this source takes a fair amount of time to setup and manage.
- **Money or cost**: Minimal or free to start if you do all the work yourself. As your list grows, you may need to pay more to maintain the list but at this stage it is likely a worthwhile investment.
- **Experience required**: This does take some technology skills to set up and maintain but you can outsource all or part of it.
- **The ability to target ideal readers of your book**: Excellent. Presumably the only people on your list are those that want to hear from you, otherwise you don't want them on the list.
- **Amazon customer reviews**: There is no sure thing but an author mailing list probably the most reliable way to get Amazon customer reviews.

- **Other benefits**: Besides asking list members if they would like an ARC of your book for the purpose of leaving a review, your list is your best option for promoting book sales. This alone is worth the investment.

 See my online guide, Getting Started with Email Marketing. http://breve.link/brc7

Source 2: Book reviewers

Primary review goal: customer reviews

When your goal is reviews on Amazon, there is no better resource to mine than Amazon reviewers themselves. Unfortunately, Amazon made that a whole lot harder in early 2018 when they removed emails from reviewer profiles.

You can still find these reviewers, but you'll have to track down their email address via social media or websites. Your success is dependent on your ability to follow online footprints.

To be sure, when you do find someone willing to review your book it can be well worth the time investment. I suggest spending a couple hours to see if it makes sense for you and your book.

Steps

1. Find your book's category on Amazon or look up popular books similar to yours.

2. When you find three to five books, look most closely at the more recently released books (the publication date is under **Product Details**) and specifically those with many reviews. The more recent reviews mean that this reviewer is more likely to remember the book and is predisposed to leaving reviews.

   a. Hover your mouse over the review box and click **See all [#] reviews**.

   b. You should see **SORT BY**; select **Most recent**.

3. Optional, but recommended: I begin by looking at five-star reviews and work my way through to those with fewer stars. Might this reviewer enjoy your book? You are also looking at each review to see if it sounds legitimate—did the reviewer spend time reading the book? "Great read" is hardly the kind of review you want for your book.

4. Advance review copy reviews. Some reviewers will say they received a free copy in exchange for an honest review. When I see this, I'll click the reviewer's name to see if they have written other reviews. If not, I move on. If they have, I'll add them to my list to look for an email.

5. As noted in three, you'll need to visit each profile to decide if the person is worth tracking down.

   a. Have they written other reviews? If yes, great! Continue.

b. Do they mention a website or social media account? If yes, visit and find an email. If not, I'd seriously consider moving on.

As you can see, this is time consuming. But it is one of the best of the ten review sources available. It's worth a shot, especially if you don't have a budget, or if you have access to someone who can help with the research.

Summary recap

- **Your time investment**: Significant.
- **Money or cost**: Free other than the cost of the books you send to interested reviewers.
- **Experience required**: Anyone can develop the sleuthing skills required.
- **The ability to target ideal readers of your book**: This may be the best source of all ten in this chapter.
- **Amazon customer reviews**: Bingo!
- **Other benefits**: Note that you can do this on any website that allows people to leave reviews, such as Goodreads, Apple, Barnes & Noble, and so on. In fact, I'd use this source if I was trying to build up reviews for my books in other online stores.

Source 3: Giveaways/discount promotions

Primary review goal: customer reviews

The idea of discounting or giving away your book—print or eBook, but usually eBook—is to build word-of-mouth awareness and get customer reviews. As a review strategy, giving away your book was highly effective in the early days of eBooks when prices were higher and supply limited. Free or cheap eBooks are still common—especially with the advent of Kindle Unlimited and eBook sale promotions—but it's lost some of its luster as a review-generating source.

Nevertheless, it remains a relatively affordable way for debut authors to reach a large group of readers quickly. It's just that instead of getting scores of reviews, you might get a handful.

Before you give up and move to the next source there are two other benefits. Many authors use giveaways and promotions with the objective of getting readers to join their mailing list. The idea is that with an email address you will be able to promote a future book, product, or service.

A second benefit is boosting the sales rank of one's book. These promotions are most frequently employed on Amazon where books attempt to obtain the coveted status of "best seller" or "#1 New Release," assuming the book sells enough copies to qualify.

These are the reasons why this source can be used repeatedly without regard to the original release date of your book.

Is this a good strategy for your book?
If you decide to move ahead with this as a review strategy, here are a few points to keep in mind:

1. The better known the author, the better the chance of their book being reviewed.
2. There is a pack mentality at work here. Lots of reviews seem to invite even more reviews.
3. Those who have a mailing list and/or social media following do better. Telling your contacts about your free or cheap book is an easy promotion to share. If some of these have already received a copy, encourage them to share your promotion with their friends.
4. People don't read and review free books as quickly as they read books they pay for.
5. As always, look for promotions that will target your ideal reader. Join the promotional mailing list you are thinking about buying for your book. For example, you can sign up with BookBub and see what kinds of books they promote to their mailing list.
6. People who get books for free can be harsher in their reviews.
7. Are you prepared to drop your price below $3 or give your book away for free?

Examples of giveaway and promotion services

Note: There are dozens of promotion services that can help you give away your book or promote a sale.

1. Goodreads Giveaway:★
   https://www.goodreads.com/
2. BookBub: https://www.BookBub.com/
3. Book Gorilla: https://www.bookgorilla.com/
4. Ereader News Today (ENT):
   https://ereadernewstoday.com/
5. kbookpromotions: http://kbookpromotions.com/

★Read more about Goodreads under Review businesses–services.

Summary recap

- **Your time investment**: Modest. Some promotion services show you availability, some don't, so you need to go website-by-website to schedule promotions for the period your book will be discounted. Or you can hire a service such as http://www.book-rank.com/ to do it for you.
- **Money or cost**: Costs range from a few dollars to hundreds of dollars. Some of these, such as BookBub, are more often used to promote book sales.
- **Experience required**: No special training needed.

- **The ability to target ideal readers of your book**: Most of the promotion websites allow you to choose the type of reader you wish to reach. (Keep in mind that they reserve the right to approve your selection.)
- **Amazon customer reviews**: Readers post reviews wherever they like but that's generally Amazon because they are the largest retailer.
- **Other benefits**: No lasting benefit other than your deal is announced.

Source 4: Traditional media

Primary review goal: editorial reviews

Many of us are consumers of traditional media such as newspapers, magazines, radio, and television. But unless you've been living under a rock these last few years, you know that most of these outlets are under tremendous pressure and have dropped or scaled back book reviews. That doesn't mean you should not try to get your book reviewed but know that it is exceptionally hard for self-published books to break through.

Like with many other PR opportunities, those who are well-known, writing about a hot topic, or connected in their local communities will find the path easier. Local stories are especially important for media today because local media needs to be relevant to their local community.

Find a local angle for your book and look up media companies in your community. Or perhaps *you* are the story. Why did you write the book? What are your ties to the community?

And don't forget about any organizations or associations you belong to. One of my clients is a psychologist and was successful in getting his professional association to write a short article about his novel.

This is really the domain of public relations professionals. The good ones have lots of contacts at just the right places. And not just traditional media, but blogs and other online outlets as well. It's a relationship-driven business so when Lisa the publicist tells her reporter contact she has a great book, the reporter listens. If you try to contact the same reporter, you are probably less likely to get through. Or it will take more work.

Summary recap

- **Your time investment**: Potentially significant.
- **Money or cost**: It depends on the media outlet but generally there is no charge. (However, be prepared for them to try to sell you advertising or exhibitor space at an upcoming event like a conference or tradeshow.)
- **Experience required**: I suggest reading about how to approach the media before you begin.

- **The ability to target ideal readers of your book**: There is no targeting with general consumer media but that's not the case if you are part of a professional association.
- **Amazon customer reviews**: This is not the goal with this source.
- **Other benefits**: You never know who is going to read a story about your book. This might lead to other opportunities such as a speaking invitation, a book signing, a partnering arrangement, or new subscribers to your mailing list. (See how I keep coming back to this?)

Source 5: Review blog tours

Primary review goal: editorial reviews

A virtual book tour, or blog tour, is like the traditional book tour except it happens online. Periodically, over the course of days or weeks, a different book blogger features something about your book. It could be an interview, an article written by the author, or that blogger's review of a book.

Arranging these tours is a lot of work! First, you need to create a list of bloggers who are willing to review books like yours. Then you need to contact each one and arrange for them to read and review your book.

Or you can hire someone to do this for you.

Blog tour organizers are individuals or public relations firms who have relationships with book bloggers. So instead of you contacting book bloggers individually, tour organizers do it for you. This has several advantages:

1. Most importantly, this saves authors (or publishers) time. Instead of manually combing through pages to find the perfect reviewers, these firms often have relationships with lots of bloggers.
2. Equally important, the book bloggers who sign up have voluntarily asked to be contacted by these tour organizers.
3. Because they have these relationships, they can often deliver results more quickly. Authors who have tight timelines should get better results.

There are a few things to keep in mind:

- There is a fee. Entry-level costs for a basic review tour can range from $25 to $150, while monthly retainers for full-service firms can run several thousand dollars a month.
- Not all book bloggers participate in tours, and you don't get to choose bloggers.
- In my experience, nonfiction is a harder tour for tour organizers to book.
- Effectiveness can vary.

For best results

1. Have a budget. You can quickly narrow down the options by eliminating firms that require a retainer. However, you do get what you pay for.

2. You'll quickly come to realize that the lower-priced review tours work best for specific types of books. There are lots of bloggers who review romance, young adult, and paranormal. At the other end are nonfiction where there are fewer reviewers (except for memoirs). Consequently, it is easier to get reviews for popular genres, which means it costs you less.

3. Quality matters a great deal. The reputation of the firm organizing the tour is on the line. Make sure your book cover is genre-specific and the text is edited.

4. Don't work with more than one tour organizer at a time. That's because book bloggers often work with more than one tour organizer. You don't want two tour organizers contacting the same blogger.

5. Contact blog tour organizers weeks in advance. Popular organizers are busy people and need time to solicit bloggers who are interested in reviewing your book. And those bloggers need advance time to read your book and write a review. In my experience you should anticipate a one- to

two-month lead time between contacting a tour organizer and the dates your tour will run.

Examples of marketing firms that run blog tours

1. PR by the Book: https://prbythebook.com/
2. Sage's Blog Tours: http://www.sagesblogtours.com/
3. iRead Book Tours: http://www.ireadbooktours.com/
4. RBTL Book Promotions:
   http://www.rbtlbooktours.com
5. Xpresso Book Tours: http://xpressobooktours.com/

Summary recap

- **Your time investment**: Easy to arrange but you will be asked to write articles and answer author interview questions. You also need to monitor the tour as it progresses and be prepared to engage with readers on the blogs featuring your book.

- **Money or cost**: Prices vary widely but are generally a few hundred dollars.
- **Experience required**: No special skill required.
- **The ability to target ideal readers of your book**: Depends on your book's genre and tour company relationships.
- **Amazon customer reviews**: Many do, but ask to make sure they will post on Amazon.
- **Other benefits**: In addition to getting book reviews your book is now permanently featured

on those blogs. This can have long-term benefits for your online presence because you and your book will likely show up in search results on websites like Google.

Source 6: Review businesses—traditional

Primary review goal: editorial reviews

I use the term *traditional* here to refer to companies that are in business to review books, and do not charge the publisher. The five examples of review businesses noted below have high standards, and their reviews are arguably the most influential because of it. Several also publish print magazines, in addition to maintaining an active web presence.

The people who read these reviews tend to be institutions and individuals who make buying decisions for libraries, schools, and retailers. They require books submitted for review to be sent months before publication date.

They consider self-published books but be forewarned—competition is fierce. The reasons I believe they accept so few books from small presses are the same reasons newspapers, television, and other traditional media don't:

1. They make money other ways, such as selling advertising. How many small presses and authors can afford these rates? A larger publisher, on the other hand, can. Longer-term relationships

matter to this group, especially deep-pocketed ones.

2. These publications know that self-published books are rarely stocked by bookstores, and instead sold primarily on Amazon and perhaps a few other online retailing websites such as BooksaMillion.com or BN.com. Why should they provide essentially free promotion for Amazon?

3. Their readers—decisions makers at institutions—are unlikely to buy self-published books.

I'm not saying you shouldn't submit your book for consideration. A well-produced book backed by a solid sales and marketing plan has a chance. But keep your expectations in line with the noted realities. Here are five examples of traditional review businesses.

1. *American Book Review*:
   http://americanbookreview.org
2. BookLife★ (*Publishers Weekly*): https://booklife.com/
3. *Booklist*: https://www.booklistonline.com/
4. *Library Journal*: https://www.libraryjournal.com/
5. *School Library Journal*: http://www.slj.com/

★*Publishers Weekly's* BookLife is for self-published books. Traditionally published books are submitted by the publisher using a different process.

Summary recap

- **Your time investment**: Each has specific guidelines you must follow and some can be quite involved, especially the advance notice required.
- **Money or cost**: There are no fees.
- **Experience required**: Little or no experience, other than assembling all the right materials.
- **The ability to target ideal readers of your book**: Each describes who their readers are and they are generally librarians, bookstores, and schools.
- **Amazon customer reviews**: Do not expect Amazon customer reviews.
- **Other benefits**: If you are trying to reach influential institutional buyers, a blurb from one of these publications carries a lot of weight.

Source 7: Review businesses—fee

Primary review goal: editorial reviews

This is a crowded category with well-known names like *Kirkus*, but also smaller businesses who have reviewers posting their review directly on Amazon, complete with a star rating. Some may charge more for faster service, but all accept virtually any book you send them.

Prices generally range from $49 to $425 (and more for faster service), so it pays to understand what you are getting for your money, and why the services from one review business might be better for your book and goals than another.

The main distinction between these businesses is whether the review is posted on Amazon as a customer review versus provided to you for use as a blurb for posting in the editorial reviews section of your book's Amazon listing.

Some say they also promote the review via their website, social media, and/or a mailing list. A few also share their reviews with industry websites used by book buyers.

As noted in the introduction to this chapter, you need to ask yourself who you are trying to impress. Amazon shoppers? Bookstore buyers? Librarians? Most self-publishers, especially first-time authors with limited budgets, will find it best to focus on customer reviews and specifically Amazon.

Also check out their stats and claims. For example, visit Alexa.com (http://breve.link/brc11) and enter the review businesses website. If the review business is claiming that your review will be seen by all their website visitors, but their visitor traffic (according to Alexa) is poor, I'd consider another reviewer if that's your goal.

Finally, several of these will allow you to "kill" the review. If you don't like the review, you can tell them to keep it private. You will still pay, but at least those harsh words won't see the light of day.

Examples of businesses offering paid reviews

(Those that post their review(s) on Amazon are noted as such.)

1. BlueInk Reviews: https://www.blueinkreview.com/
2. Dog-Eared Reviews (Amazon):
   http://www.dog-eared-reviews.com/
3. IndieReader (Amazon and editorial):
   https://indiereader.com/
4. *Kirkus Reviews*: https://www.kirkusreviews.com/
5. Self-Publishing Review:
   https://www.selfpublishingreview.com/

Summary recap

- **Your time investment**: You simply fill out forms.
- **Money or cost**: All these businesses charge a fee.
- **Experience required**: None.
- **The ability to target ideal readers of your book**: You have no control. They choose who reviews your book.
- **Amazon customer reviews**: Some post Amazon customer reviews.
- **Other benefits**: A few are recognized by the public, such as *Kirkus*, and those reviews may impress shoppers or third parties. Reviews are also often promoted on their website and perhaps to their followers.

TIP: Some authors choose these reviewers (and hybrid reviewers in the next section) because they want to hear what professional reviewers think of their writing. I won't wade into the debate about whether that's justification for buying these reviews, but I do think you need to be careful if that's the purpose. Consider the feedback just one reviewer's opinion and know that some reviewers are not as competent as you might think. Watch for outlier opinions and consider it valid feedback only when shared by several reviewers.

Source 8: Review businesses—hybrid

Primary review goal: editorial reviews

Hybrid book review businesses offer a limited number of traditional no-fee reviews as well as paid reviews.

The paid reviews generally are for any book, subject to the policies of the business. Free reviews must meet other criteria. For example, a request for the free Foreword Review must be submitted four months before publication date.

Each company has their own guidelines, some of which have nothing to do with book categories and more to do with how the book was published.

For example, Chanticleer Book Reviews states that to qualify for a free review, the publisher must publish books by multiple authors, and the authors must not have any responsibility for the cost of producing or distributing the book.

As with traditional no-fee reviewers, authors and publishers have no influence or control over these reviews. If your book is accepted for a no-fee review, it will be published. Most of these companies permit sponsored or paid reviews to be withheld from publication.

Do these companies offer free reviews as "bait" to sell you a review? Perhaps, but we know that they do publish reviews that are not paid for.

Examples of hybrid reviewer businesses

1. Chanticleer Book Reviews: https://www.chantireviews.com/
2. City Book Review: https://citybookreview.com/
3. Foreword Reviews | Clarion Reviews: https://www.forewordreviews.com/
4. Portland Book Review: http://portlandbookreview.com/
5. The Children's Book Review: https://www.thechildrensbookreview.com/

Summary recap

- **Your time investment**: You simply fill out a form.
- **Money or cost**: Be prepared to pay, especially if you want a guaranteed review.

- **Experience required**: None.
- **The ability to target ideal readers of your book**: You have no control. They choose who reviews your book.
- **Amazon customer reviews**: Some post Amazon customer reviews.
- **Other benefits**: A few are recognized by the public, such as *Foreword Reviews*, and those reviews may impress shoppers or third parties. Reviews are also often promoted on their website and perhaps to their followers.

Source 9: Review businesses—services

Primary review goal: customer reviews

This is one of my favorite methods for proactively seeking reviews for any book.

- The businesses in this section do not review books; they help you reach reviewers. That means there is an arms-length relationship between your book and the person reviewing it.
- You are not buying reviews. Your payment, if any, is for a service in the form of access to a network of readers. You are basically offering your book and waiting for someone to read and review it.
- The reviewers self-select. In theory, reviewers ask for books they'd like to read. This helps ensure that reviewers read only those books they are interested in.

- They are affordable. Costs can range from free (LibraryThing) to less than $400. I know $400 seems rich, but in all cases with businesses in this category the promise is that you'll receive more than one review. For those with a budget to spend on reviews, these can be a huge time saver.

A few downsides or cautions

- No kill option. Unlike some of the paid services where you can kill a negative review, these services provide no control over the content of a review, or whether it is even posted.
- Patience is required. It's difficult to control the timetable as to when a review is posted. Like other services, advance planning is needed, especially for popular categories with popular services (such as the romance category at Hidden Gems Books).
- Some reviews can be harsh. As stated earlier, your Addressable Audience is always the best source of reviews; they'll come more easily, be free, and generally skew more positive. The readers in this group don't know you and some can be more than candid. As always, do everything you can to match your book to the right reader. It also helps to have thick skin.

Examples of businesses offering review services

1. Goodreads Giveaways: http://breve.link/brc8
2. Hidden Gems Books: https://www.hiddengemsbooks.com/
3. LibraryThing: http://breve.link/brc9
4. Prolific Works (formerly Instafreebie): https://www.prolificworks.com/
5. Reedsy Discovery: http://breve.link/brc10

Summary recap

- **Your time investment**: Fill out online forms.
- **Money or cost**: There is usually a fee but some are free.
- **Experience required**: None.
- **The ability to target ideal readers of your book**: The reviewers choose books they are interested in so in that way you know they have an interest in your subject.
- **Amazon customer reviews**: Reviews are most likely to be posted on Amazon as customer reviews.
- **Other benefits**: Generally no.

 TIP: Some businesses used to sell lists of Amazon reviewers. Since Amazon removed contact information from profiles in early 2018, such lists are likely old and out of date. Buyer beware!

Source 10: Book bloggers

Primary review goal: customer reviews

I've dedicated the entire next chapter to bloggers considering the time and experience required, and the possible benefits if you do commit to using them.

Summary recap

- **Your time investment**: Potentially significant although you can easily contact bloggers periodically in your spare time.
- **Money or cost**: They do not charge for reviews but some will charge a small fee if you want your book read more quickly.
- **Experience required**: No special skills unless you want to automate part of the process.
- **The ability to target ideal readers of your book**: Excellent.
- **Amazon customer reviews**: Most post reviews on Amazon.
- **Other benefits**: All post reviews on their website. Most also promote their reviews on social media and some have mailing lists. Many also post their reviews on other websites such as Goodreads and LibraryThing.

5

Bloggers

"In this digital age, book bloggers are the golden child of self-published book publicity."
— Marika Flatt,
Founder, PR by the Book

There are several reasons to break out book bloggers into their own chapter. Here's why they are popular:

1. **Volume**. There are hundreds, if not thousands, of book bloggers.
2. **Variety**. Reading interests range from the obscure (books about the "beat generation") to the broad (young adult [YA] and romance are two of the largest genres).
3. **Approachability**. A high percentage of bloggers review self-published books.
4. **Free**. Most bloggers do not charge a review fee.

5. **Value**. Reviews are usually posted in multiple locations (Amazon, Goodreads, etc.) and the blogger promotes the review on their website and via social media.

Ah, but finding the needles of bloggers in these haystacks of reviewers is, well, a mission that requires a plan, time, and perseverance. Many have thrown their arms up in frustration. On the other hand, stories about blogger reviews boosting an obscure book to success are not uncommon.

In defense of book bloggers, consider their oft-cited complaints about working with self-published authors:

1. **Excessive requests**. Popular bloggers are inundated with review requests.
2. **High author expectations**. Bloggers resent the badgering some authors resort to when launching a new book.
3. **Frustration with quality**. The best ones also review traditionally published books and that's the standard you are being held to. Some have given up and have stopped reviewing self-published books due to poor quality.
4. **Impatient authors.** Many book bloggers are hobbyists. In this essentially volunteer role, they may take weeks or months to read a book. Most have jobs, families, or are in school and sometimes they need a break. Or something

unexpected happens to delay their commitment to read a book.

5. **Lack of gratitude**. After hours of reading, writing the review, and posting it publicly, the least authors can do is promote the review and thank the reviewer. Many authors do thank them, but some don't.

It's not hard to address the above issues. Just follow these simple ground rules:

1. Approach only those bloggers who state an interest in your genre or subject matter. This is explained on their website.
2. Follow their directions. Never send a book unless they ask for it.
3. Respect their time and don't argue with their review.
4. Submit only quality books. Unedited books won't be considered. Worse, the reviewer may express his or her dissatisfaction publicly in the review—if it gets that far.
5. Contact them thirty to ninety days before your book's release date to improve your chances of being accepted. If that is not possible, be flexible with your expectations.

TIP: Most bloggers use the information you submit and/or what they find online to decide whether or not they will review your book. They look at your book cover, read about the book, study your online profiles. Your online presence must look professional. This includes your Amazon author profile, your book's listing in the online store(s), your website, and your social media accounts.

Quick-start guide

As I mention previously, you need a plan and part of that plan includes good record-keeping. Trust me, thirty minutes into a search for bloggers will leave your head spinning.

"Didn't I just look at this website? I think I sent her a query email, or did I? Wait, no, it was a blogger by the same name, but the website address was .net, not .com."

It gets confusing fast, and you don't want to waste time. So, here's my recommended step-by-step guidance for approaching bloggers. (How to find them is coming right up!)

1. Create a process and record-keeping system for tracking who you plan to contact, and the status of each request. See my Reviewer Outreach Checklist in Bonus 1.

2. Assemble your book's details. (Also explained in the Reviewer Outreach Checklist.)

3. Visit one of the resources listed under the heading **Sources of book bloggers**. Look for reviewers who review your type of book.

4. Research three to five of those bloggers to start. Once you get your system refined this will go much faster and you can expand the number of blogs you are researching.

5. Now visit their website to review their submission requirements.

6. Look for terms like "review policy," "review submissions," or their About or Contact pages for instructions. These are usually in the menu or a sidebar on their website. Do not contact bloggers unless your book matches their interest.

7. Record the ones you plan to contact (step 1) and contact them according to their instructions. Follow up according to their instructions. Some will give you a timeframe, some say they will contact you if they are interested.

8. Repeat steps three through five as you have time. There is no advantage to blasting out dozens of queries in one sitting. In fact, contacting bloggers in smaller batches will help you keep better track of conversations and be more human in your outreach.

This is essentially a sales process; you are trying to convince these reviewers that your book is worth their time to read.

No specific submission instructions? Write a great query email

Some blogs do not have submission instructions, so your only choice is to send an email or fill out their contact form. Putting our marketing hat on, we're going to send a message that respects their time and gets their attention.

- **Subject line**: This is the most important thing you'll write. Say "Book review query" and then as few words as possible describing your book relative to their interests. (Their past book reviews are the best indicator of their interests.)
- **Addressing/salutation**: Personalize your email by using their first name, not sir/madam or "Dear Blogger." Their social media accounts or comments on their site are good places to look for first names.
- **Message body**: Introduce the book in a way that appeals to their interests. Make it easy to read, and to the point without extraneous details. If your book is like a book they previously reviewed, mention it. If you have a notable blurb, include it. Include a link to the cover if possible—perhaps the book is on Amazon, or there is

an image on your website. (But no attachments at this stage!)

- **Signature block**: Your name, your relationship to the book, a link to your website, and your email address.
- **Proof**: Check spelling and grammar. This is a reflection on your book. Don't use emojis, slang, or acronyms like LOL.

Putting it all together

[Subject line] Book review query: WW2 alt fiction with romantic interludes

Dear Jen,

I found your blog when I was searching book bloggers interested in romance and I understand you also like history. I'm excited to submit *Shadows and Joy*, a behind-the-warfront romp between two lovers from opposite sides of the war.

It is 312 pages and available in paperback, Mobi, EPUB, or PDF—your choice. I'm flexible on dates but my release date is [fifty days from now].

[reader blurb if you have one, for example: "Jennifer Doe from Doe Reviews said '*Shadows and Joy* was unlike any other historical fiction book I've read. Fast paced, believable, and titillating. Well-written too.'"]

You can click here to see the cover: [link to book on John Doe's website]. I also have an excerpt available here: [link to excerpt on John Doe's website]

Can I answer any questions or send you a copy? If so, please tell me what you require.

Thank you for your time,

John Doe
Author of *Shadows and Joy*
www.authorwebsite.com
Johndoe@gmail.com

Author etiquette: The art of approaching book bloggers

1. Approach only those bloggers interested in your book's category. If you don't follow their directions, most will delete your email and never reply. Reaching beyond your book's category will not get you reviews—don't waste your time.
2. Quality matters. Reviewers are inundated with books to read. Some have stopped reviewing self-published books due to poor quality, others because of self-published authors not following their requirements (see number one). A polished book is more likely to be considered and gain a favorable review.

3. Make your pitch friendly, respectful, and to the point. Address them using their name. It is a sign you read their blog. Follow their instructions—never send a generic query or form letter.

4. Lead times can be long and schedules tight. Bloggers are essentially volunteering to read your book. Manage your expectations—plan ahead, be flexible, and don't be demanding. Many bloggers clearly state how or if you should follow up after you've made initial contact.

5. The reviewer is doing you a favor. Make getting your book free, easy, and convenient. Do not expect the reviewer to buy your book or pay for shipping. (They have too many other books to read! See number two.)

6. Don't expect them to love your book. Some won't post a critical review and instead will provide feedback on why they didn't like it. Some won't explain themselves. Some will indeed post their honest opinion. Avoid potential issues by approaching only those reviewers who enjoy your genre.

7. Be gracious and say thank you no matter the outcome (email or postal mail). Remember, you are building relationships because you might be back with a follow-up book. Kindness, just like rude comments, has a way of living forever on social media and on websites. Reviewers can and do research authors.

In summary, follow the Golden Rule. Treat reviewers the way you would like to be treated.

Anna-Marie Abell: What happens when you don't follow directions

It is very important to research and make sure the blogger reads your genre. This may seem like a no-brainer, but it goes further than that.

Almost all blogs have a page that tells you what they accept *and* their pet peeves. If you don't adhere to this, then you could get a really bad review. For example, I had missed on one blog I submitted for that they *hate* cliffhanger endings (which I have) and so my review was less than pleasant.

I soon learned that those who hate cliffhangers REALLY hate cliffhangers, so a book review can go from a five-star to a one-star simply for having it. Had I paid more attention, I could have avoided a bad review (which can drastically take your star rating down on Goodreads and Amazon). Bloggers DO post bad reviews everywhere, so that is why you have to be diligent that you are contacting a blogger who reads and likes your specific genre.

Also, not only should you make sure the blogger reads your genre, but you should also check out a few of the reviews they have written. There are some bloggers out there who love to rip apart books. There are not a lot; most do provide honest reviews. But it is in your best interest to make sure you don't contact a blogger who writes harsh reviews or is often negative.

• • •

Anna-Marie Abell is the author of *Holy Crap! The World is Ending!: How a Trip to the Bookstore Led to Sex with an Alien and the Destruction of Earth*

FAQs: Frequently asked questions

An occasional frustration I hear is that a book blogger is not currently accepting books to read, they are too busy to receive unsolicited requests, or the blogger may simply be uninterested. That's the nature of book blogging, so move on to the next book blog. Here are a few other questions I hear:

Q: How do I know whether a blogger is worth my time to contact?

First, accept that it is the blogger who is doing you a favor, not the other way around. But given your limited time, and assuming a large source of blogs to approach, there are a few key indicators of high-quality book bloggers. Consider these collectively and use your best judgment.

Also keep in mind that a blogger who is just starting out may become more popular in time, so starting a relationship with him or her now may benefit you in the long term.

- How frequently do they post reviews? A high frequency of quality book reviews often leads to more visitors, which makes that blogger more influential.
- What is the website's Alexa ranking? The lower the number, the more popular the website: http://breve.link/brc11
- How many social media followers do they have on their different platforms?
- Does the website have a high number of inbound links, and how high is the Domain Authority? Both are measured by the free Moz Open Site Explorer tool: http://breve.link/brc12.

Q: Do all bloggers review all types of books?
No. In my experience most bloggers are interested in genre fiction with romance and YA dominating. Within nonfiction—and a fraction of all bloggers will consider nonfiction—memoirs and biographies dominate.

Q: What is the difference between Kindle and Mobi?
Many reviewers use the terms interchangeably to refer to Amazon eBooks that are read using Kindle apps, Kindle devices, and Fire tablets. Anyone can read a Mobi file using a free Kindle reading app from Amazon. Some bloggers say Kindle when they

prefer you to gift them your book from the Kindle store. Ask if it isn't clear.

Q: This is taking a lot of time. Is there an easier/faster way to get reviews?

No, unless you have a budget to pay blog tour organizers to present your book to their list of reviewers. And there are many review businesses who review books for a fee. You either spend your time or spend your money.

Sources of book bloggers

Unless you hire a marketing or book PR professional you're going to have to find book bloggers on your own. In addition to the obvious choice of using Google, there are online directories, directories of directories, and at least one published book (ahem, mine, see next section).

Google

Using Google to find book reviewers is challenging because it is harder to keep track of your progress and it can be overwhelming. However, the results will be top blogs depending on how you are searching. This is where it helps to know some Google search hacks that help you zero in on the most relevant results.

Here are my favorite ways to narrow search results:

- Use quotes marks to find exact phrases. This helps you find a multi-word term. For example, "romance book bloggers" will find results that contain that exact phrase.
- Use a minus sign. Put a minus (-) in front of a word to exclude results that have that word. For example *-romance* will exclude search results with that word.
- Use the word *OR*. *OR* (it must be in all caps) combines terms for a broader search. For example, *biography OR memoir* will find results containing both terms.
- Find even more hacks here: http://breve.link/brc13

TIP: Jason Ladd has perfected a sophisticated strategy for approaching book bloggers using technology tools and Google. He shares his techniques in his book *Book Review Banzai* and you can read my review of it here: http://breve.link/brc14

Directories

Directories of book bloggers are another option. Here are five I've used, including one that I publish.

1. The Indie View: http://breve.link/brc15
One of the oldest online resources for book reviews.

2. Book Reviewer Yellow Pages:
http://breve.link/brc16

The Book Reviewer Yellow Pages has been around for ten years and is best known for publishing an annual paperback and eBook of blogs. The current directory has 200 blogger listings, as well as listings for other review resources. There is also a free online directory of about 2,000 blogs. (Disclosure: *I am the publisher of this directory and some of the information in the directory is included in this book.*)

3. The Book Review Directory:
http://breve.link/brc17
This site offers a number of services such as advertising, publishing services, and paid book reviews. The link takes you to the directory of bloggers.

4. Book Blogger List: http://bookbloggerlist.com/
This directory is one of the largest. As is true of all directories, some listings are old or are no longer accepting books.

5. Reedsy Book Review Blogs: http://breve.link/brc18
Reedsy's directory is in its second year and it has a number of features that make it easy to use. It has a mixture of listings for review businesses, like *Kirkus*, as well as blogs run by individuals. Not all listings accept indie books.

Book bloggers; blogs and bloggers

What's the difference between book bloggers, and blogs and bloggers? The book blogger writes blog posts about books while the blog or blogger treats books as just one of many topics they write posts about. For example, Huffington Post and Medium are considered blogs and I consider myself a blogger.

For the author, it doesn't matter who reviews your book as long as the reviewer loves it and shares their opinion with as many people as possible.

Besides the focus on non-book topics, here are two other points about blogs and bloggers:

1. A blogger may be more interested in receiving a free book to review than a book blogger. Books are not their focus so there is less competition in this regard for their time.
2. In my experience, book bloggers tend to be fiction oriented whereas bloggers tend to be more nonfiction oriented.

 Finding bloggers to review your book might take a little more research, but that research may be something you've already done, especially if you write nonfiction. Look for influencers who blog about your topic or subject matter.

How to find bloggers

What organizations or influencers are closely associated with your subject or topic? The crucial follow-up question is how many of these review books or would consider reviewing a book? Here is a process to help get you started:

Obviously Googling your topic with the word blog and blogger in the search term works. For example:

- Trekking in Nepal blogs
- Trekking in Nepal bloggers
- Retirement investing bloggers
- Nutrition blogs
- Auto repair blogs

Depending on the volume of results received, you may want to narrow your searches. Use quotes around specific terms, or the minus sign to remove unwanted terms from results. This often brings up a whole new set of results.

Once you find a few bloggers to approach, follow the advice in the book blogger section. Check if there is a fit, contact them to see if there is interest, and follow the rules of etiquette.

Also, established bloggers sometimes include a "blog roll" in their website's—a list of other blogs they read and may have a relationship with. This is a rich source of related blogs so visit each one to see if there is a fit.

Cherie Kephart: Start early and stay organized

I started contacting bloggers and reviewers three months in advance of my book release date. I looked to determine whether the reviewer was active in the last few months and gave honest and objective reviews. I kept a log of everyone I contacted, how I contacted them, the dates, and what their responses were. It took a few months to go through the list and to make all the personal connections.

Know that a lot of people you contact simply don't have the time and won't respond to everyone. It is nothing personal. And only approach those reviewers and bloggers who take your genre of book, otherwise, you are wasting your time and theirs. Besides, it is best to contact those who enjoy the type of book you read, which increases your chances of getting reviewed, and perhaps a more favorable review at that.

One blogger loved my book so much that I made it to her top 20 books she has read in 2017. Also, from her promotion of my book I was contacted for a radio interview.

• • •

Cherie Kephart is the author of *A Few Minor Adjustments: A Memoir of Healing.*

Chapter summary

1. Every website with a blog is a potential reviewer. Approach only those that match the audience for your book.

2. Approach each blogger (or website that publishes blog posts) with humility and with an answer to the question: What's in it for them? Will their readers benefit or enjoy learning about you and your book? Do you have a way to promote a review they write to your own network? Perhaps you might offer a bonus they can give away to their readers—copies of your book, a gift card, or a free consultation.

3. Follow their instructions for submitting books or articles, and be responsive to their requests. They are doing you a favor, not the other way around.

4. Don't stop looking for opportunities. The reason your book launch is a good time to contact bloggers is because your book is new and newsworthy. Look for other newsworthy opportunities to contact blogs and bloggers in the months and years ahead: something happens in the news that relates to your book, the anniversary of its release, a milestone has been reached, a significant endorsement is secured.

6

Endorsements/Blurbs

"I always used to wonder about this genius of a man wanting or needing reassurance."

— Robert Bernstein,
former Chairman of Random House,
sharing how Theodor Geisel (Dr. Seuss),
insisted on reading his new books
out loud to Mr. Bernstein to get his
immediate approval.

Favorable comments and kind remarks from people that matter, matter. They matter to our readers; they matter to the media, retailers, and other gatekeepers who can help us sell books. And let's face it, they matter to us.

If Chapters 4 and 5 are about whom to approach, then this chapter is about how to use what those people say to impress people. You want to gather feedback about your book from the right people and organizations and then try to shape what they say in such a way as to meet your goals.

Blurbs go by many names in publishing—testimonials, endorsements, review quotes, and editorial reviews—and they all mean the same thing: someone influential, who has relevance to the audience of your book, has spoken highly about your book and/or you.

The source of the blurb can be a customer or editorial review, or it can be something written specifically for this purpose by a noteworthy individual or organization. Sources also include statements by fans or the media.

Regardless of the source, it is short and to the point. In fact, all the better if you have a collection of blurbs each making a different point.

I argue that a blurb can be just as powerful as an editorial review, if not more so.

- It won't cost you money the way an editorial review usually does.
- The blurb writer could have more relevance to your readers than the name of the editorial reviewer or organization.
- If your goal is to influence readers, you have to wonder how many are going to read a 250-plus word review.

You can also upload blurbs yourself to the key platforms that accept them, for example, Amazon and IngramSpark.

At the same time, Codex Group CEO Peter Hildick-Smith, whose company works with all the major publishers, has tested book covers with variations of blurbs, including covers with no blurbs. A Codex survey asked shoppers two questions that relate to using blurbs as a promotional tool:

1. "Do you care about who's doing the blurbing, and is it somebody who really matters to you?"
2. "Is it something that's really bringing some value to your understanding of the book?"

Their research shows such blurbs have a minor influence on buyers: "Just 2.5 percent of participants discovered it through the recommendation of their favorite author; about 1 percent of them were persuaded to buy a book because of such a recommendation."

Still, that didn't stop Walt Whitman from including Ralph Waldo Emerson's praise (apparently without permission) to promote the second edition of his debut book of poetry, *Leaves of Grass*. "I Greet You at the Beginning of a Great Career," Emerson wrote in his letter to Whitman.

Nor did it dissuade Ernest Hemingway from plastering no fewer than six blurbs on the cover of

his first commercially published book in the U.S.
(Source: http://breve.link/brc19)

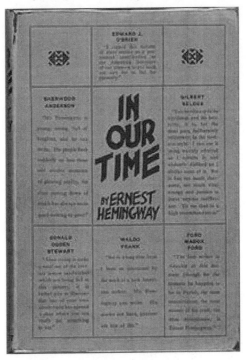

Why blurbs are worth getting

It is never too soon to begin thinking of people
who may speak kindly about your book. In fact, it
isn't unheard of for an agent or publisher to ask for
the names of potential blurbers when considering a
manuscript for publication.

This usually means someone your audience would
recognize, but it can also be an organization such as

an association, publication, or other media outlet. It comes down to who you are trying to impress.

In some ways you might find it easier to get a blurb than to get a review. This may seem odd, but my theory is that people feel a review on Amazon is more public than those same words printed inside or on a book. It is also more work.

Consider this:

- A blurber does not have to have an Amazon account, login, and figure out how to post a review (not that this is hard, but it does take time).
- A blurber often feels a review must be longer than their short paragraph praising your book.
- Some blurbers will ask the author (or publisher) to write the blurb on their behalf, or use a pre-written blurb provided to them. This obviously isn't possible when writing book reviews.
- A blurb (generally) is not a permanent entry on a website, whereas a review is a public record that can "live forever."

Consequently, it is easier to turn a review into a blurb than to get the blurber to post their feedback as a review on Amazon.

As implied in the Codex research cited earlier, blurbs may or may not help sell your book. They certainly won't hurt, but there are many other ways to invest your time for marketing—and blurbs are indeed a form of marketing.

How do you plan to market your book? Do you see an opportunity for third parties to help you reach readers?

More likely, blurbs help to validate a book in the eyes of third parties. The right blurber can open doors. For example:

- If you want to be interviewed on a podcast, a blurb from someone the host knows will likely carry weight.
- A children's book with a blurb from *Library Journal* may indeed impress a decision maker at Baker & Taylor, a top wholesaler to schools and libraries.
- The target audience for your new romance book will no doubt know and pay attention to a blurb from a bestselling romance writer. (And it's great marketing for the blurber in this case as well.)

Broadly speaking, when thinking about individuals who might lend their name in support of your book, I divide them into two categories:

1. People and organizations whose names your prospective readers, the media, or book industry professionals might recognize.
2. People who will write a review, ideally on Amazon.

That's what we're going to discuss now; how to be strategic. Whom to approach, how to approach them, and how to use what they give you.

Blurbers—pre-launch outreach

Like reviews, authors never stop collecting blurbs for their books. Always be on the lookout for a new blurb you can add to your book promotions and online book profiles.

Since blurbs are a form of social proof, the attribution for the blurb can be as important or more important than the blurb itself. Otherwise you could write your own blurbs and attach a made-up name, right?

What are we looking for? Any or all these attributes:

1. A name your readers recognize.
2. A quote that speaks to the author's qualifications or expertise.
3. A quote that praises specific elements or benefits of your book.
4. A name recognized by third parties, such as bookstore owners or someone in the media.

Also keep in mind that the name of the organization a person is associated with or their position in that organization can carry more weight with readers than the name of the blurber. This is especially true for nonfiction books.

Traditionally published authors benefit from the assistance of their publisher. But any author can draw inspiration from what some indie authors can achieve working on their own. Consider these examples from bestselling indie books:

Getaway Girl, Tessa Bailey (romance)

- Two blurbs by *New York Times* bestselling authors, who also happen to be self-published: Mia Sheridan and Skye Warren
- Five blurbs by book bloggers
- One blurb by a "Goodreads Reviewer"

Miracle Morning, Hal Elrod (self-help)

- Two blurbs by *New York Times* bestselling authors Tim Sanders and Ivan Misner (who also has a self-published book)
- One blurb from someone whose qualifications are "TV show host, author, and Teen Behavior Expert"
- A blurb by Rudy Ruettiger, the subject of the film about the Notre Dame football player by the same name

How to Market a Book, Joanna Penn (self-publishing)

- Five blurbs by individuals who are notable self-publishers themselves
- One blurb from a traditionally published author who is also a noted publishing consultant

As you see in these examples, there are no political leaders, industry titans, or reviewers for major media organizations. From what I could determine, there is just one traditionally published author out of eighteen blurb writers and yet each of these books is a self-published bestseller.

The individuals these authors selected to blurb their book appeal to the readers they are targeting. There is not a single quote from a review business such as *Kirkus Reviews*.

Several years ago, we published a directory of San Diego micro-breweries, compiled and edited by a beer expert writing for the *San Diego Reader*. All twelve of the author's blurbers—people working for well-known local breweries—wrote about his expertise and made no reference to the actual book. Here's a representative example:

> Brandon Hernandez is a well-respected journalist and member of the San Diego craft beer scene. In the three years I have known him, he has fervently promoted new and established breweries through his expert reviews.

Blurbs can also address benefits or perceived deficiencies and, in that way, prepare the shopper for what to expect. In this regard a key role of the blurb is to attract the right reader. Not just any reader, but readers who would enjoy the book. What good is it to sell a book only to have a disappointed reader leave a negative review, or speak poorly of the book to their network? (Re-read the Perry Marshall quote at the top of Chapter 2.)

Think of each blurb as filling a specific role. The blurb can highlight special features, plot elements, characters, or it can mention a similar bestselling book.

> Blurbs aren't just for books; they can also be used to compliment the author. For example, my client Dr. Mardy Grothe, the author of seven quote anthologies, uses this accolade in his bio: ". . . described by Fred Shapiro, editor of The Yale Dictionary of Quotations, as 'one of the most profound and popular quotation book authors of all time.'"

Timing: when should you start?

The most important time to solicit blurbs is before your book is released as part of your pre-release marketing plan. As such, it is imperative that the solicitation period be given as much time as possible. Two factors influence how much time to allow:

1. Are you already connected with influencers?
2. How approachable are the people you are trying to reach?

Clearly, there is a direct correlation between how well you know someone and how easy and fast it will be to get their endorsement. I'm sure some of us have relationships where all we need to do is write the blurb and send it for their approval. But that's rarely the case in most situations.

Usually the process is more involved and there are several steps and factors that will impact the speed of a response. Assign the time you think each of these steps will take:

1. Research the names of people you want to approach.
2. Find their contact information.
3. You may need to go through an intermediary such as an administrative assistant, agent, business manager, or their publisher. The higher the level of the person you are trying to reach, the more challenging and time consuming the process will be.
4. Wait for a reply, follow up again, wait some more.
5. If they are willing to consider it, you need to send them the book or a manuscript (more on how to do this below).
6. Wait some more while they consider your request.
7. If they accept, they will probably need time to read it.
8. Once read, they need to write the blurb.
9. If you want to request a change that requires their approval, wait some more.

In my experience the process of soliciting a blurb is going to take one to six months. Again, depending on the circumstances.

Now multiply this by the number of people you are trying to reach—and add in time to work on other marketing and publishing tasks—and you can see why advance planning and extra time is imperative.

Soliciting blurbs
ASK!

Seriously, in many cases—assuming you are approaching people via a personal connection or within reasonable reach (probably not Oprah)—you'd be surprised by the positive reaction. Timing also matters, as does the relevance of your book to the person you are approaching, and obviously the quality of your book (writing and presentation).

Your book needs to be worthy of blurbing. The higher you aim, the stronger the book must be.

- It does help if you are connected in some way, even if it is a few degrees of separation. Maybe you are connected via another person and they are willing to reach out on your behalf.
- Are you in the same line of work or members of the same association? Do you share a hobby?
- When you overlay your life/contacts/interests with theirs, where are the connections?

If you are like most authors and think, "Who am I? Why would they blurb my book?" you're not alone. We all feel this way.

But guess what? They don't approach this the same way you do. What if the shoe was on the other foot? What if all sorts of people were asking *you* to endorse *their* book? Imagine all their readers seeing your name under a blurb—a social signal that you are a highly sought-after authority. Hmm, that sounds like marketing. Yes, their blurb helps you but it also helps market the blurber as an authority, which further enhances yours. A virtuous circle of mutual support.

At the same time, don't waste time overreaching. This is essentially influencer marketing in that you want someone more famous than you to recognize you as being important. Assuming I'm approaching people I don't know, I'd look for people who are one or two status levels above my influence level.

As I noted in Chapter 5, Book Bloggers, get your online presence in order before you begin reaching out to people for help. Assume they will do their due diligence online.

What does your online presence say about you? If someone Googles your name, or looks at the links in your email footer, what might their impression be?

If they are at or just above your status, they are flattered. Much above that and they may already have all the fans they need. In fact, they want to move up their own ladder in influence.

For my first book, I thought a blurb from a well-known self-published author would be helpful so I reached out to Cheryl Kaye Tardif, bestselling author of *How I Made Over $42,000 Selling My Kindle eBooks*. It was a cold email, so I had no idea if she would even reply. She responded within a day, asking me to send a PDF of the book. Less than two hours later—before I even sent the PDF—I received a second email that read: "I took a look at your website and I don't think I'll have a problem blurbing your book."

TIP: What do I mean by status levels? Compare the popularity of your website to theirs. Compare the number and engagement of your social media followers to theirs. How often are they in the news relative to you? How many books have they written compared to you?

Metrics like these are popularity signals. It isn't to say that an author who scores zeros on all the metrics should not approach an important influencer for a blurb. I'm simply suggesting that your ability to reach someone influential should take these factors into consideration and you should manage your expectations accordingly.

Sources and methods for identifying potential blurbers

Soliciting blurbs is nothing more than networking. Who do you know and how good are you at reaching out to meet new people?

While it's impossible for me to give you a specific plan, I can share sources that have worked for other authors.

1. Writers and instructors you met at writing conferences.
2. Social media connections such as LinkedIn, Facebook, and Twitter.
3. Blurbers for books similar to yours. (Visit the book's page on Amazon and look in the editorial reviews section for that book's blurbers.)
4. Celebrities that have publicly expressed a passion or interest about the topic of your book, or whose background is relevant to your book.
5. Authors of similar books.
6. Authors who share the same agent or publisher.
7. Authors published by your publisher. (But be aware that while readers may be impressed, the media and book selling professionals tend to view these blurbs as less impressive.)
8. Organizations—businesses, associations, not-for-profits, a religious organization—that are aligned with the subject matter of your book. Note that LinkedIn is a terrific resource for looking up leadership teams for this exercise.

9. Read the acknowledgements of books related to yours. Who did the author thank? Some of these individuals may also be interested in your book.

10. Ask members of your publishing team about their connections. Perhaps they are willing to make an introduction.

11. Lastly, tell your personal network of friends and family the names or types of people you are interested in reaching. Brainstorm names and ideas with them.

Protocol and reminders

In all cases the same protocol applies whether you are approaching your best friend or a stranger.

1. Allow plenty of time and never rush or make unreasonable demands. The lead time you need depends on how well you know someone or the layers of gatekeepers between you and that person.

2. Follow directions. If someone says they want a finished book, or for you to contact them in two months, do what they ask. If they don't accept unsolicited books, don't send one in advance.

3. Think in terms of levels. For example, if you are targeting three people who are peers, go after the one you think is most approachable. Once that blurb is in hand, approach the next one and

reference the blurb you just received. People like to know they are in good company.

4. Always keep in mind that this is just one aspect of your marketing plan and should not be pursued at the exclusion or reduced effort on other marketing efforts. Once you have a handful of good blurbs, perhaps it is time to focus on other marketing efforts. This is especially true for those of us with large networks or where networking like this is easy.

TIP: If you have a lot of good, potential blurbers, ask them all. Some may not follow-through in time or may give you a blurb that is less powerful than another. The best ones will be used in the most visible manner and those that don't quite meet your objectives can still be used on a praise page on your website.

Do you send a file, a printed book, or both?

One of the great misconceptions of new authors is the idea that their book will be pirated and shared widely for free, or worse, the story or idea copied by others. I can't say this won't happen, but the odds are slim. Consider these facts:

- An average of more than 3,000 new books are released every day. The idea that only yours is unique doesn't seem reasonable.

- In all likelihood, the people you are contacting are ethical.
- If someone loves your book so much that they share it with someone else, consider it word-of-mouth advertising. This very thing happened to Adam Mansbach's *Go the F**k to Sleep* and it went on to international bestseller status.

For these reasons, I don't consider the sharing of early versions of books to be a risk. In fact, in my experience it's done nothing but help. You may even get valuable early feedback that can improve the book and/or the marketing of it.

With that in mind, what should you share? My rule of thumb is to share the book in whatever format the blurber (or reviewer) wants it and that I have available. That can take the form of Microsoft Word, a PDF, Kindle eBook, EPUB, or a printed book.

I talk above piracy in more detail in Chapter 7, Advance Review Copies.

How to format blurbs

A blurb has value only because of someone's or an organization's reputation. Your job is to respect that reputation and support it to the satisfaction of the blurber.

When it comes to formatting the blurb, it is as much about what *not* to do than what to do when presenting it to the public.

Attribution can be as important as the blurb itself

If the blurber does not specify how their blurb should be attributed, or credited to them, ask. Most do specify, and it is their name, and a reference to their company, business, or the name of a book they've written. But sometimes it is a mixed bag.

I asked an industry acquaintance to blurb my second book and the attribution was longer than the blurb itself! It consisted of his name, business focus, and an industry affiliation. It wouldn't have been so hard to use it except he is not widely known and the blurb itself was underwhelming.

In this case I saved it to my blurb file and used it on my website along with a bunch of other blurbs. Like the penguins in the movie *Madagascar* are famous for saying, "Just smile and wave, boys. Smile and wave."

Editing blurbs: never change intent or meaning without asking

Here are three rules if you want to shorten the blurb you are given.

1. Never edit a blurb in a way that misrepresents the blurber's intent.

2. Always respect how they want to be credited and follow their wishes. While you may reduce a blurb down to its pithy core point, never do the same to their attribution.
3. Unless they have given you permission otherwise, go back to the blurber and ask them to approve your change.

TIP: I like how *Kirkus Reviews* describes what you can and cannot do. Here are their three rules:

1. If words are omitted from a quote, ellipses must be inserted in their place.
2. No words may be added to the review.
3. The integrity of the review may not be altered.

Be consistent and clear when formatting

You have flexibility when formatting blurbs—there are no rules other than to be consistent and clearly separate the look of the quote from the attribution.

The quote can be in italics, or with quotation marks, but generally not both. The attribution can be the opposite of this with an em dash (a long dash) in front.

Head to your bookshelf or library to see how other books format blurbs, or your designer will know what to do. Don't overthink it.

How to use blurbs

As I said earlier, blurbs are marketing tools. Here are ten ways they can be used, not all of which are appropriate for all types of blurbs.

1. On the front and/or back cover of your book.
2. At the very beginning of your book.
3. In media kits and on collateral such as bookmarks.
4. On your book's sales page on online stores (on Amazon this area is called Editorial Reviews).
5. In your website and social media postings.
6. In your bios, including those used for social media accounts.
7. In your email signature.
8. In email newsletters to your mailing list.
9. In letters or emails to potential partners, retailers, wholesalers.
10. In emails to other blurbers when you ask them to blurb your book! (In fishing, this is called chumming the water.)

Obviously if you have one blurb, or very few, the decisions are easier. Also, you don't have to include blurbs in all of those ten applications in the above list and you can always add them as they become available.

Remember that traditionally published books from large publishers have teams of people collecting these so a request from a known publisher to a leading authority is more apt to get a positive response. Be creative in who you approach and look for people who might benefit from blurbing your book.

Where to put blurbs in books

Looking back at the list of ten possible places to use blurbs, you'll notice that it is in order of permanence. That is, adding blurbs to books is usually done before they are published and then rarely updated due to the work involved.

Printing collateral that has blurbs, such as bookmarks and postcards, is also something done infrequently. Items four through ten are more easily managed because they are electronic. Sales pages, websites, and bios are updated as new and more noteworthy blurbs are collected. If you are pitching a guest post to an influencer or an interview to a media outlet, it is simple enough to grab your most impressive blurb for that specific circumstance.

Blurbs and book covers

The best advice is to look at books from comparable authors to see what they do. Most self-published books stick with back cover blurbs.

One of my clients uses a single blurb for the back cover of the paperback and puts several more inside the book. Her hardcover on the other hand has a list of ten blurb excerpts on the back of the dust jacket, and the full blurbs listed on the opening pages in the front of the book.

The reason for a different treatment for the hardcover is that the dust cover's front and back flaps have the bio and book description so that frees up space on the back.

What about the front cover? Well, do you have someone or an organization with such broad name recognition that you don't mind its detracting from your other cover elements? Perhaps after the book has gained some standing on its own can a blurb be added to the cover.

It reminds me of a client who was fortunate enough to receive a pre-publication blurb from a well-known author. It was quite a coup, so she wanted it on the front cover. About two weeks after publication I received an urgent email to take the book down until the blurb was removed. I can only imagine what was said and wonder if my author's assumption cost her a friendship.

The author never asked permission to use this individual's blurb.

Inside the book

If blurbs are included inside, they are placed at the beginning of the book, in whatever order you deem appropriate. You, of course, will be sending a copy of your book to the blurber with a note of appreciation so keep this in mind.

There are many ways to title this page, or you can leave a title off. "Praise for [book name]," "What people are saying about [book name and/or author]." As always, let comparable books be your guide.

How to use blurbs (editorial reviews) on Amazon and IngramSpark

Amazon and IngramSpark are notable because they allow self-publishers to add editorial reviews directly to a book's sales page in selected online stores. Traditionally published authors can also do this on Amazon (via AuthorCentral), but you need to ask your publisher for help with other online stores.

Adding editorial reviews on Amazon

The reviews listed under the Editorial Reviews section for a book's listing on Amazon appear there by manually entering them using AuthorCentral or are placed there automatically by select review businesses (for example, *Publishers Weekly*, *Booklist*, and *School Library Journal*).

You can add or edit Editorial Reviews for each format that is listed for sale or on pre-order. For example, my client Jill Thomas' book *Tales from the*

Trance was traditional published. Her hardcover was available for pre-order, but not the Kindle edition. I was able to add editorial reviews for the hardcover before the release date but had to wait for the Kindle to be available before adding editorial reviews to that edition. It works the same way for self-published books.

Pre-release view, hardcover only book format

Hardcover only: Pre-release view of a book's AuthorCentral page.

Live-release view, Kindle and hardcover formats

Here is the view of Jill's AuthorCentral page five days later. You manage Editorial Reviews for each format separately.

1. Login to your AuthorCentral account: http://breve.link/brc20.

2. Click Books in the top menu, then select your book. (If your book isn't there, click the **Add more books** button and follow the instructions to add your book.)

3. In the Editorial Reviews tab, the first heading should be Reviews—click edit.

4. Repeat step 3 for each format (Kindle, hardcover, etc.).

Additional notes about editing Editorial Reviews using AuthorCentral

- In a few instances I've found it necessary to ask Amazon for help in formatting Editorial Reviews. When that happens, they turn off your ability to make further changes. I think this is because their HTML editor is a little wonky—at least that's my experience. Be prepared to experiment, or just give up and ask for help.

- As previously noted, some reviews are placed here automatically. In fact, those are added under their own heading under the top-level heading of Editorial Reviews. If that is the case with your book, you won't be able to edit or remove those. Amazon states: "In order to keep Editorial Reviews objective and informative, we rely on many sources to provide content for this section. We work to create a diversity of opinion on our site, and this may include negative reviews, when they arise."

- Managing your AuthorCentral profile for other country-specific Amazon stores isn't as easy as it is for the U.S. store. In my experience you need to use their contact forms to have the changes made by Amazon staff.

Adding editorial reviews on IngramSpark

If you are using IngramSpark to distribute your book to stores such as Barnes & Noble, they too have a field where you can enter editorial reviews. In their system these are called **Review Quotes**.

Login to your account and select your book. You will find the field to enter **Review Quotes** in the section titled **Categorize Your Book**.

In my experience it takes a couple weeks for these to appear on BN.com (Barnes & Noble) and Indigo. ca, the large Canadian book retailer. Whether the reviews appear on other retailer websites that IngramSpark distributes to is up to those retailers and is not something IngramSpark guarantees. For example, my books on Books-a-Million and Powell's do not show **Review Quotes** even though they are entered in IngramSpark.

Three helpful suggestions from IngramSpark about Review Quotes

1. Include two to eight positive review quotes. These should be from a variety of sources and should highlight different aspects of the book.

Ideally, reviews will come from people and publications known by and influential with potential buyers.

2. Each quote should be brief (no more than fifty words each). Provide excerpts from longer reviews.

3. List the most powerful or effective review quote first.

Chapter summary

While most often thought of as something to get before your book is published, blurbs are something you never stop collecting. For this reason, it is important to continue to ask for them and then keep track of them when someone does say something nice about you or your book.

1. Ask people who your readers might recognize as an expert in what you have written about:
   a. An individual with name recognition, and/or,
   b. An organization related to your book.

2. Approach blurbers as soon as you have a book to share. This is usually your ARC. But it can also be your manuscript.

3. Keep track of everything. I use a Word document that has a three-column table for date, blurb, and attribution.

4. Try to ask a range of people and use a variety of blurbs in your marketing. You don't want every

blurb to say the same thing. You also don't have to use every blurb you get.

5. It takes longer than you think, and not everyone will be willing to write a blurb.

7

Advance Review Copies of Books—ARCs

"An ARC is primarily a book marketing tool."

— Jane Friedman

Throughout this book I've referenced creating and distributing advance review copies of books for the purpose of soliciting feedback and reviews. But what exactly does that mean? Let's start by defining ARCs.

An ARC is simply your book in any format and in any state of completion.

- Format examples: Microsoft Word, PDF, Mobi (Kindle), EPUB, paperback, hardcover.
- State of completion: An unedited manuscript or the fully edited, designed and printed book.

Examples of possible ARC recipients:

- Foreword writers
- Beta readers
- Peer review readers
- Potential blurbers
- Book reviewers

Galley vs proof vs ARC

In today's modern publishing landscape, these are essentially one and the same. Before we had PDFs and print-on-demand (POD), publishers would print galleys and use these to solicit reviews and blurbs. Those galleys generally consisted of a plain cover with the name of the book and interior pages of text, without any formatting or professional typesetting.

Today, everything is electronic. It's also far easier, faster, and cheaper to use email. Books are usually drafted electronically, and the push of a button turns them into a PDF. It's also simple and cost effective to print copies of a book using POD.

Why go through the extra step and cost of creating an old-fashioned galley? You don't.

Which format to share and when to share it

The questions then become, which format do you share and when do you share it? The factors that influence the answers to these questions are:

- How well do you know the person you are approaching? In my experience, the better you know the person, the less concerned you need to be about how complete and well-edited your book is.
- What format is your reviewer, blurber, or foreword writer asking for? Some people are fine with a PDF; some want a finished book. Others may want a Kindle formatted eBook.
- What is your budget? If readers want a printed paperback and your book isn't quite complete—you may be waiting for illustrations, an index, or a final proofing—you might need to print ARCs for them and then complete the remaining publishing steps before finalizing the book for printing or eBook programming. This is most likely going to cost more money.

Oftentimes it comes down to timing. If the launch date is weeks away it's probably makes most sense to provide finished books to reviewers.

Practical advice for most books

I've found that most people willing to write a blurb are happy to get a PDF, something a word processing program like Word or Google Docs can produce. These writers want a general feel for your book and the PDF is sufficient. Depending on how well you know them, it may not even have to be edited. Ask them.

The people you are approaching for reviews, and services that distribute your book to reviewers, are another matter. They are nearly always going to expect to choose between an eBook format (Kindle or EPUB) or paperback. They also expect your book to be edited.

How to turn your ARC into a marketing tool

For those who are planning far in advance and have a defined marketing plan, the back cover of the printed ARC should be enhanced with information that appeals to the media and booksellers instead of readers.

- Reduce the amount of text and space devoted to the book description.

- List a publicity contact (phone, email, and Twitter account, if available).

- Provide a bulleted list that highlights your marketing plans. These marketing plans should include your plans to market to the industry, not just readers.

- Be sure the author bio speaks to the author's qualifications and accomplishments, and note if they have media and marketing experience.

- Share ordering and distribution information. The people who receive your ARC want to know if the book will be available from outlets other than Amazon.

- Include details about the book such as all available formats with prices and ISBNs, book categories, number of pages, and trim size. Even if this information is on the copyright page, you want to summarize it here. Don't make your recipient work to get it.

Finished books vs books labeled as ARCs

Books provided in any format in advance of their release date are considered to be ARCs. But traditionally, publishers labeled these copies as ARCs which allowed them to get the unfinished book to reviewers months before the release date. It also made the books unsaleable because these ARCs had labeling on the cover, on the interior pages, or both—and no retail barcode.

Whether or not you add ARC labeling is entirely up to you. Carolyn Howard-Johnson, the author of *How to Get Great Book Reviews Frugally and Ethically* advocates sending finished, final books to reviewers. She points out that being able to resell a book—or to keep it for one's library—is kind payment for someone taking time to review your book.

Indeed, I have on my shelf a copy of Pat Flynn's *Will It Fly* that I bought used. It has a personal note from Pat to someone who helped him with his book: "Thanks for your help with *Will It Fly*.

Looking forward to working with you for many years to come."

When my company produces ARCs for reviewers, we advise our author-clients to follow one of two approaches depending on the release date of their book and their personal preference.

1. If the book is within about six weeks of its release date, we recommend sending the final book.

The reason is that any extra copies can be sold or given away as gifts. Another consideration in this case, if we are offering the book for pre-order, is making sure the final version of the book is uploaded to the IngramSpark system in case retailers order copies in advance of the release date.

2. If the release date is longer than about six weeks, we're more comfortable adding ARC labeling.

In this case we're getting two versions of the book ready, so we need extra time. The first version has ARC labeling, the second is the final book with ARC labeling or branding removed.

Options for ARC labeling

One or all four of these techniques can be applied to a printed book to brand it as an ARC:

1. Add "Advance Review Copy" to the cover.
2. Add "Advance Review Copy" to each page of the interior.

3. Add a watermark to interior pages (text that is in the background, behind the print).
4. Do not include a barcode with an ISBN on the back cover. (This is possible when using Ingram-Spark, and automatic when printing proofs using KDP Print.)

Unauthorized sharing or piracy

I don't generally consider unauthorized sharing or piracy a problem for many authors, especially new authors. But I want to add two considerations here.

Popular authors, or those writing on a broadly popular subject, are more likely to experience unauthorized sharing of their book. These authors know who they are and take precautions before sharing their books.

For example, they may distribute only print editions of new books and/or be highly selective about who receives advance review copies. If they make their ARC available in eBook format, it may be limited to a service that has digital file controls in place, such as NetGalley.

Regardless of your popularity, you may hear that your book is available from a strange website as a "free download." On the surface, this looks pretty scary. You'll see a picture of your book, the title and perhaps the description, and download now buttons. It's a scam. These are phishing websites designed to harvest emails from people looking for a deal. That usually means us—I know because this has happened to me for each of my books.

These websites have automated the scraping of eBook retailers to grab key information and put it behind an email registration page. New books are prime candidates because people are actively searching for them online.

I can only speak for myself when I say that I know for a fact that my book is not available for download from these websites. Further, if someone is so desperate to save a couple dollars, they are not the ideal reader for my book.

Do you need to send the complete book?

Once again, how much of your book to send is a judgment call on your part. Most often, people want to see the entire book in some form as discussed above. But others may be satisfied with an outline or a few chapters.

A practice that is common for larger books, especially those with lots of images such as illustrations or photographs, is to create what's called a BLAD, a book layout and design or as basic layout and design.

These consist of the cover and select interior pages that represent what the finished book will look like. They are used as a marketing and sales promotion tool because they are less expensive to produce and distribute than the full book.

They can also be produced in advance of completing the entire book, an important consideration because books with lots of illustrations or pictures are more complicated to design.

 To learn how to produce an ARC using KDP Print, see my article here: http://breve.link/brc21. For help creating ARCs using IngramSpark, see my article here: http://breve.link/brc22.

8

Being Strategic: 7 Ways to Make Your Life Easier

The definitions of strategic are:

- Relating to the identification of long-term or overall aims and interests and the means of achieving them.
- Carefully designed or planned to serve a particular purpose or advantage.

I recall a phrase my coach used when I was a few months into starting a consulting practice. I had all sorts of plans and expectations but was feeling blue about my progress. Gary said that I was "living on hope but dying from despair."

I've worked with dozens of new authors who experience the same arc of emotions. Part of this is driven by outsized expectations ("There is no book like this!" or "All my friends love it!") and sometimes driven by their past successes in life (successful entrepreneurs, CEOs). Regardless of how you became a writer, regardless of your budget, regardless of the power of your story, I believe it is possible—necessary even—to step back from your book and do some strategic planning.

Approach your *hope* for success with humility, planning, and patience. There *are* things you can do to help improve your chances of success. And with each step upward you get a chance to reach the next level.

I can't say much about your humility or patience. But I can share seven strategies that have helped other authors. One is super-simple, one you probably can't entertain right now, two are painful thoughts, and the other three will require a level of effort you didn't think was necessary.

Be strategic. Skip these at your peril.

1. Price eBooks aggressively

A mistake I see new indie authors make is equating price to the level of work or investment they made in the book. Or they price it based on what they perceive as the value it delivers. (Traditionally published authors are usually at the mercy of their publisher when it comes to pricing the book.)

New authors usually need to earn that higher price. Some may be so famous that this is easy. But for most of us, we should be more focused on getting the book read than maximizing the profits of a book that will sell few copies at a higher price. You must establish value in the eyes of a shopper, and even large brands sometimes have problems doing this.

Take pricing eBooks, for example. In 2010, the *Harvard Business Review* decided to carve several long (regular-length) books up into what they called "Short Cuts" and sell each of these "chapters" for $3.95. They thought it was a clever way to turn a $15 ten-chapter book into a $40 purchase.

Poor reviews and dismal sales hastened their removal. People saw though their money-grab for what it was.

Around the same time, Stephen King's publisher released his *Blockade Billy* priced at $4.99 for a 112-page eBook. Read what this two-star reviewer had to say:

> My main problem with Blockade Billy, however, was the price tag. . . . the story itself should have been released as a 99 cent download for Kindle, included in a magazine or even (horrors!) just given as a freebie for buying a real book. So why wasn't it? GREED.

And this:

> While I don't necessarily equate the value of a good story to be proportional to length, I do expect a fair price and to be provided relevant information as I make a purchase. Great books are worth more to me than the cover price.

That leads me to a second fact of life when it comes to pricing: most self-publishers have a more difficult time commanding the same prices for their books as traditionally published authors. This is especially true for new authors, or authors whose names are not synonymous with the subject of their book.

Finally, under promise but overdeliver. Meaning, if you produce a high-value, well-edited, professionally presented book for a lower than average price, chances are that readers are going to reward you with appreciative reviews. That's exactly what I did when I released the 9th edition of *The Book Reviewer Yellow Pages*. As one five-star review noted, "And at the current price of .99 USD, this is a real bargain."

With eBooks, you can price aggressively and increase it as you and the book become better known. The low price will attract and reward early buyers, setting the stage for sustainable sales into the future.

2. Ask for a review at the end of your eBook

Pointedly asking your reader to review your book is a best practice that developed with the growth of eBooks. Including it is certainly prevalent with self-publishers, and you don't see it as common practice in print books, but "it doesn't hurt to ask." If you think it is ill-mannered or desperate, consider how many businesses actively encourage customers to leave a review on Yelp.

You have two options for implementing this:

1. Add a generic request—do not mention an eBook store.
2. Add a store-specific request for Amazon in your Mobi file, and a generic request to the EPUB file. (Amazon specifically because its reader reviews are by far the most popular with shoppers.)

You can also take option two a step further by linking your request to the review page for your book on Amazon. This is a multi-step process, so I'll explain how further below.

What to say and where to add it

There is no standard phrase or wording to follow; use common sense and your own voice. Here are a couple versions I've come across as a reader that made me feel compelled to leave a review.

You can place your request on a page with a title such as "A Small Favor" or don't title it at all. In either case I suggest adding it immediately following the end of your primary content and before back matter such as endnotes and about the author.

Generic version 1:

Thank you so much for reading my book. Won't you please consider leaving a review? Even just a couple of sentences would be a huge help. It really does matter! Please visit the online store where you bought this book and leave a review there.

Generic version 2:

If you enjoyed this book, please leave a quick review (it only takes a couple of minutes). Reviews help us authors know whether our books were helpful, give us motivation to keep writing, and help others learn about our books.

Referencing Amazon specifically

As with any sales pitch—and that's what you are doing here, you are selling your reader on the idea of leaving a review—the easier you make something for the customer, the more success you'll enjoy. In this case, mentioning Amazon and linking to the review page for your book, removes all barriers.

- The probability is high that he or she bought your eBook from Amazon.
- You can add this wording to the specific file you upload to Amazon.

- Amazon makes it easy to link to your book's review page.

Before continuing I need to share two important points. One, never ever link to Amazon in a book you want to sell in Apple Books. They will reject your file. Other stores may have the same policy so simply avoid doing this.

Two, I've noticed that Amazon has been adding their own "leave a review pitch" at the end of books. They say "Before you go. . ." and then show you five empty stars with and invitation to "Review this book on Amazon and Goodreads." Depending on the device you are using, pressing a star takes you to a page to enter a headline and your twenty+ word review. On other devices you may enter the text of your review right where they ask you to review the book.

Steps to reference Amazon

If you are simply mentioning Amazon by name, then it is as easy as editing your request to say Amazon instead of the generic wording in the prior examples. Linking to your review requires editing your eBook file or coordination with your eBook programmer to do this for you.

First you need to know the ASIN, or Amazon Standard Identification Number, for your eBook. This is like an ISBN in that it is unique to the specific edition of your book. It is also used only on Amazon.

The ASIN is assigned by Amazon when your Kindle eBook is listed on Amazon, whether the book is for sale or for pre-order. Obviously adding the link to the review page inside your eBook is more easily done before your book is available to the public and pre-order is necessary to do that.

First find your ASIN on your product details page:

Product Details

File Size: 1466 KB
Print Length: 160 pages
Simultaneous Device Usage: Unlimited
Publisher: PartnerPress.org (March 17, 2016)
Publication Date: March 17, 2016
Sold by: Amazon Digital Services LLC
Language: English
ASIN: B01BX7Q02K
Text-to-Speech: Enabled
X-Ray: Not Enabled
Word Wise: Not Enabled
Lending: Enabled
Enhanced Typesetting: Not Enabled
Amazon Best Sellers Rank: #66,635 Paid in Kindle Store (See Top 100 Paid in Kindle Store)
   #1 in Kindle Store > Kindle eBooks > Law > Intellectual Property > **Patent, Trademark & Copyright**
   #1 in Books > Law > Intellectual Property > Patent, Trademark & Copyright > **Copyright**
   #73 in Kindle Store > Kindle eBooks > Reference > Writing, Research & Publishing Guides > **Publishing & Books**

Then add "B01BX7Q02K" to the end of this link:

- http://www.Amazon.com/gp/customer-reviews/write-a-review.html?asin=

So it looks like this with the ASIN placed at the end:

- http://www.Amazon.com/gp/customer-reviews/write-a-review.html?asin=B01BX7Q02K

3. Gift books to reviewers

Never expect a reviewer to buy your book. Buying someone a book is an incredible motivator in that they feel an obligation to reciprocate.

This is obviously easier and less expensive with eBooks, but I don't get bothered if someone asks for a print copy. It is so difficult to get reviews, and they are so valuable, that when someone says they will write or consider writing a review, I do everything possible to make it easy for them to do so.

My preference in this case is to send my prospective reviewer a digital gift card to buy my book. It takes less than five minutes and they receive it via email. This way their review is labeled as a verified purchase.

Trust me, a few dollars per legitimate review gets you a huge return on investment.

4. Ask contributors for help

Ask everyone who contributed to your book to help spread the word. This includes people who provided written material such as a foreword or guest chapter. Or maybe there was an illustrator or photographer.

Generally, these individuals are credited in your book, so they have a vested interest in helping it succeed. They also have a network of contacts who may be willing to receive a copy for purposes of writing a review.

(I'm not suggesting you ask them to write a review.)

TIP: Contributors named in your Amazon book listing can get their own free AuthorCentral profile. AuthorCentral profiles can contain a contributor bio, photos, and even link to the contributor's blog if they have one. Contributors with AuthorCentral profiles are hyperlinked to their profile thus giving shoppers a chance to learn more about the contributor.

5. Length matters

Admittedly, it is a little late to be talking about a shorter book when you are planning a review strategy. But if you are currently working on a book, or planning a new one, know that reviewers do consider length when evaluating a book to review.

Early in the process of publishing a client's book I noticed that it was 235,000 words. Not only would a book of this length take a long time for an already busy reviewer to read, but it would be expensive to print. We would have had to price the paperback over $20 just to make a couple bucks and at that price we knew many readers would pass on it.

On the other hand, Mark Coker, the founder of Smashwords, shares research that indicates readers love longer books and we know that long audiobooks are among the most popular on Audible. In these cases, it may make more sense to skip the paperback and take your chances with reviewers. This is often the case with genre fiction. (http://breve.link/brc23)

Keep in mind that the longer the book, the greater the commitment required from the reader—will they even finish it? And as I said before, when it comes to asking book reviewers to review your book, a shorter book is an easier pitch to make. (In fact, some review services charge more for longer books.)

6. Attract the ideal readers first

In Chapter 2, I talk about a strategy of approaching reviewers in a specific sequence. What do I mean by *ideal readers*? They are people who enjoy the subject matter of your book or like your style of writing.

Are they hard to find? They often are for new authors. That's why it is so important for authors to have mailing lists and social media connections. These connections need less convincing to read your book and write reviews. The established author on the other hand no doubt has some type of loyal following which makes the task easier.

Given my emphasis on the ideal readers, why is this so important to attract them vs. any reader?

1. Reviews from your network tend to be more favorable. They know you and are less inclined to

be negative. If they don't like the book, they may not say anything.

I recall getting an email from a reader who received an advance review copy of a client's book. He respectfully declined after reading the book rather than share his negative comments publicly.

It reminded me of the old saying, "if you can't say something nice, don't say anything at all." I'm not saying it is wrong to refrain from leaving an honest opinion or we shouldn't leave negative feedback. My point is that in this early stage of a book's release your reviewers are more likely to follow the approach of this fellow and just pass on leaving a review.

2. Referring back to The Paradox of Publicity research cited in Chapter 2, the expectations of readers who would otherwise not be an ideal reader could be high. Disappointment with your book can lead to less-than-favorable reviews.

3. Like other retailers, Google, and social media services, Amazon tracks what we do online. They use this information to show us books like the ones we've already purchased. The insider term for this on Amazon is *Also Boughts* and your goal should be to have your book be seen among books comparable to yours. Amazon is helping

you market your book by showing it to people who like books just like yours.

For example, looking up Joanna Penn's *How to Market a Book*, a shopper would see the following books (as of the date I'm writing this). This has a way of increasing sales for your book, which also helps Amazon sell books.

It's not a good sign if the Also Boughts are not similar to your book, or if the Also Bought list is short.

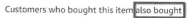 Customers who bought this item also bought

Story Genius: How to Use Brain Science to Go Beyond Outlining and...
› Lisa Cron
★★★★☆ 240
Paperback
$10.87 ✓prime

Launch to Market: Easy Marketing For Authors [Write Faster, Write...
› Chris Fox
★★★★☆ 131
Paperback
$8.99 ✓prime

How to Write Dazzling Dialogue: The Fastest Way to Improve Any Manuscript
› James Scott Bell
★★★★☆ 387
Paperback
$11.39 ✓prime

Register Your Book: The Essential Guide to ISBNs, Barcodes, Copyright, and...
› David Wogahn
★★★★★ 30
Paperback
$11.95 ✓prime

How to find ideal readers

Okay, I've convinced you of the importance of marketing your book to ideal readers. This begs the question, how do you do this? It's the $64,000 question every author asks so let me give you a few ideas to get started, some of which are discussed further in this book.

1. Start a mailing list and continuously encourage people to join it.

2. Use social media. People that follow or connect with you are far more likely to be open to receiving book announcements. By the way, you don't have to wait for them to buy your book or contact you. Be proactive and contact them. I've used a social media consultant to contact a client's Twitter followers who seemed likely to read and post a favorable review (although this was not a requirement).

3. Use Amazon Ads to target readers of comparable books.

4. Use Facebook and BookBub ads to target readers of comparable books.

5. Contact reviewers of comparable books. This can be time consuming because you need to find a name, and then locate his or her contact information. But the resulting reviews can be golden.

6. Put your book on sale (free or ninety-nine cents is best) and use a book promotion service to notify their list about your book. These services maintain email lists of people interested in specific book topics so your book will be promoted to readers who have asked to be contacted about books like yours.

7. Make sure your metadata describes your book accurately. This means using relevant book categories and keywords and ensuring your book description accurately describes your book. Never try to trick someone into buying your

book. A disappointed buyer could leave a negative review.

In some cases, we are *positioning our book* to attract ideal readers. In other cases, we are *proactively seeking* ideal readers. Review again the advice I share in Chapter 2 about The Book Review Journey.

7. Go where reviewers like to post

Amazon is big, but it isn't the only place reviewers post their book reviews (and many post reviews in more than one location). In fact, some book reviewers refuse to post there. It's also a fact that you never know where someone will learn about your book, even if they end up buying it on Amazon.

I surveyed 557 book bloggers about where they post their book reviews and discovered all sorts of non-Amazon locations for reviews. Here is a summary of the results:

Goodreads	210	38%
Amazon	199	36%
BN	49	9%
LibraryThing	21	4%
Kobo	8	1%
All others (37) combined	70	13%
Amazon, Goodreads, Audible		75%

The clear take-away from the survey: Make sure you have your book listed on Goodreads and

LibraryThing—especially before publication date—
so readers can post reviews.

This is easy to do simply by signing up for free
accounts.

Chapter summary

1. Price your book fairly, especially your eBook (if
   you have a choice). Be competitive relative to
   comparable books and overdeliver on the reading experience.
2. Create a link to your review page and share it via
   email when someone says he or she liked your
   book.
3. Always give books to reviewers free, ideally via a
   gift card. This is one of the least expensive marketing investments you can make.
4. Ask contributors if someone in their network
   would like a review copy.
5. Be mindful about length.
6. Approach ideal (target) readers first. Make sure
   your book description is written to attract the
   right buyers.
7. Go where the reviewers are. For example, make
   sure your book is listed on Goodreads and
   LibraryThing.

9

Writing and Publishing Book Reviews

"The fact is, most people do read reviews to select their reading material. Reviews do have a positive or a negative influence on whether or not a person buys a book. Hence, reviewing is a serious responsibility, one reviewers shouldn't take lightly."
— Mayra Calvani,
co-author, *The Slippery Art of Book Reviewing*

This chapter was never in the original outline for this book. I thought it wasn't relevant—the last thing a review-seeking author is thinking about is writing reviews for another author's book. Or so I thought.

But feedback from other authors changed my mind, as did reflection on my own experience writing reviews.

- Published writers told me they understood how hard it was to accumulate thoughtful reviews, so they wanted to help other authors.
- I heard from authors who said they understood how writing reviews enhanced their own brand and made them and their books more visible to potential readers (marketing!).
- And as I noted in the preface, writing reviews can lead to unexpected opportunities.

Five reasons to write book reviews

Perhaps you feel the reasons for writing book reviews are still a little squishy and not relevant to you. Or maybe paying it forward is not your thing. Here are four tangible reasons I hope change your mind.

1. Experts write reviews

Expert status is earned by carefully grooming how we position ourselves publicly. In book publishing we call this a platform. It is not binary; a switch—yes or no, on or off, expert or amateur—it happens incrementally over time. And one of the ways to build your expert status is by writing thoughtful book reviews for books where you can demonstrate experience and authority.

Here's an exercise: open the Sunday edition of the *New York Times*, *Los Angeles Times*, or the Saturday edition of the *Wall Street Journal*. Find the book reviews and read the bios of the people who write those reviews. In many if not most cases, the writer has written a book that is relevant to the book they are writing about. The reviewer earned that expert status and are now using it to further enhance their platform.

Ask yourself: Is it possible to write a book review and publish where my target reader will see it? This could be a trade publication or website, regional publication, national media, or an association publication.

You don't have to be an expert in a subject area to write a review, but the closer your background and qualifications align with the review you are writing, the more you are perceived as an expert.

2. Book reviews are content for your blog or other outlets

Some blogs would not exist without book reviews; book bloggers being the prime example. For others, such as me, longer reviews are part of my blogging strategy (see the next section). An expert who is willing to share their opinion about a related book is someone readers of that subject matter will pay attention to. Done right, someone searching Google for this author's book will come across your book review and perhaps some magic will happen.

3. Get free books

Authors, especially new authors, are desperate to have their book read. Even established authors understand the importance of early feedback and reviews so their publisher will often list the book on services like NetGalley and Edelweiss where the book is available to read for free. Keep reading—I talk about sources for books to review.

4. Meet new people

One of the best ways for a new author to jumpstart their writing career is to buy and read books by other authors in their genre, and then contact that author about their book. It's basic networking. The key is to do it with the right intentions and not expect or demand reciprocation. It does take time but if you are writing in that genre, shouldn't you be reading books like yours?

The above approach is proactive; you purposely select authors and books to review and then find a way to contact and perhaps become friendly with this author. It's also possible that the review you write might encourage someone reading it to contact you.

I recall the story of David Meerman Scott, author of *The New Rules of Marketing & PR* and a fan of Bob Marley's music, reviewing one of his albums. After the review was posted, the producers of a Marley documentary read the review where Scott had referenced being at the concert where the recording took place and that he had photographs. They contacted him about using the photos, Scott agreed, and the producers gave him credits in the film.

5. Get paid to write reviews

We're now seeing more than one million books published each year and many authors have the money to pay for reviews. We've already talked about the ethics and logic of paying for reviews, so I'll just point out that there is lots of money flowing to businesses that accept payment. Are their reviewers paid? Do those business owners make money? Of course.

There is money for those interested and skilled in writing reviews and I've noted a few resources below.

What are your objectives? Why write reviews?

I imagine what you are saying now is, "All this sounds good but who has the time?" It's an important question and the answer to which you need to be clear about before considering reviewing a book.

For some people—book bloggers, for example—the goal may be to spend time on a hobby they enjoy. They love books and this is a way to talk about what they read, meet new people, and get free books. Authors looking for reviews of their own books—you reading this book and me writing it—have much different goals.

Speaking for myself, my reviews fall into three categories that I describe this way:

1. **Strategic reviewing.** I look for books on subjects I care deeply about by authors who have a noteworthy reputation regarding their book's subject matter. These are generally authors who I follow (via Amazon, BookBub, their blog, etc.) so that I'm notified when they have a new book.

   I immediately read their book and write a thoughtful review, a review that I hope helps other readers. The strategic part comes into play when this review becomes voted up or in Amazon's case, shoppers click the "Helpful" button after reading my review. In this way I trying to position myself as an *expert*, as noted earlier. I was able to do this with Fauzia Burke's *Online Marketing for Busy Authors* where my review is currently the first one shown to shoppers.

   I will also post these reviews as blog posts like I did for *The Perennial Seller* by Ryan Holiday. I used this series of posts to qualify for Reedsy

Discovery (see Chapter 4, source 9). And as I note in Bonus 2 at the end of this book, a publicist found it and asked if I would review her client's book.

2. **Contributory reviewing.** I can't always be among the first to write a review for a new book in a subject area important to me, but I can still contribute for all the reasons stated in *strategic reviewing* above. I finish the book and write a review at a less breakneck pace in this case, and I try to make it just as thoughtful.

3. **Casual reviewing.** I also write reviews of other books I enjoy, novels: books on history, biographies, art, and travel. But these reviews are much shorter and I only write them if I feel I have a point to make that I think other readers might find valuable or the book was particularly interesting in some way. This also has the benefit of broadening my review profile such that Amazon, Goodreads, and others don't somehow flag me as a shill for authors in my strategic focus areas.

Know your own objectives and be deliberate about the books you review, the speed at which you review them, and the methods you use to publicize your reviews.

Finding books to review

You certainly don't need anyone's permission to write a customer review. The more difficult thing in my mind is choosing the book to review, assuming you are reviewing books for reasons other than the sheer joy of reading.

You can go searching for books, or you can wait for authors to seek you out, which takes more time. Here are bunch of ideas to get you started with a focus on the methods and places to find books for what I call "strategic reviewing."

1. **Amazon Author Page.** Visit the author's page (click their name under their book's title) and scroll down under their bio. There you will find a heading that says "Customers Also Bought Items By' and the names and usually photos of similar authors. Explore these authors and don't forget to check their author page for similar authors.

2. **Goodreads.** Find a book similar to yours and look for the books listed under the heading "READERS ALSO ENJOYED" and click on "See similar books. . ." to explore similar authors. Note: Some less popular books may not have enough data to display a list so look for more popular books.

3. **Amazon "Also Boughts."** I talked about this in Chapter 8, and there is a screen shot there as

well. You have two ways to use this. Find a book that is like yours and scroll down to the headings:

a. Customers who viewed this item also viewed.

b. Sponsored products related to this item.

4. **Find books by category.** Visit the book categories of online stores and check for books and authors. Research those that interest you and approach the author or publisher.

5. **Join NetGalley and Edelweiss** as a reviewer. Both companies have listings of forthcoming books that publishers want reviewers to read and review.

6. **Start a blog** or begin posting reviews on your blog. But don't wait for Google to bring you authors and publishers. Speed up the discovery of your blog by submitting it to the directories mentioned in Chapter 5 and the blog tour organizers mentioned in Chapter 4, source 5.

7. **Join an author's mailing list.** Many have launch teams and are eager to find readers willing to read and review their books.

How to write a review

You finished a book and now you are ready to write a review. Let's begin with a list of considerations and steps relevant to content and length. I'll follow this with an interview with a reviewer who reviews books for Midwest Book Review.

1. **Where will the review be posted?** I consider this the first decision to make because it dictates length and style. Possibilities include:
   - Goodreads: Length doesn't matter. In fact, all you need to leave is a rating. Most of the reviews are written in first person and are not much longer than a paragraph with many being a few words (if any are used at all).
   - Retailers, for example Amazon: Amazon requires a rating, a headline, and the review itself. The minimum length of reviews varies depending on the device you are using. For example, there is a one-word minimum when using a PC but from a Fire tablet the minimum is twenty words.
   - Your blog: Length entirely up to you.
   - Other outlets (see below): They have guidelines and you can study reviews written by others.
2. **Ethics and disclosures.** Acknowledge free books and relationships. See Chapter 3 for details.
3. **How long should it be?** This is dictated or influenced by where your review will appear, as previously noted.
4. **How many stars should you assign?** Beyond the obvious advice of being honest there is the fact that many shoppers will discount the top and bottom of the scale and focus on the middle ratings figuring they are more balanced. A rating

in this range, they hope, will bring them more readers (and helpful votes in the case of Amazon).

I've also heard people say that they don't review books they didn't like. This is often in response to criticism that their ratings lean positive. Only your conscience can guide you in this case but more important in my mind are subject lines, not to mention the contents of the review.

5. **Writing headlines (subject lines).** I consider this the second most important step when writing a review (the first being the review itself). If you want people to pause and read your review, you'll usually attract more readers with a compelling headline. What few words will grab someone's attention and make them want to read your review? Here are a few examples:

Short (too short?)	Descriptive or intriguing
• Nice summer read • I really liked it • Informative • Bestseller • Fantastic thriller! • Very good read • Not my cup of tea. . . • Skippable	• This book changed my life and could change yours. What is stopping you from reading it? • Chris Voss is an impressive guy, BUT. . . • Terribly bad, will actually make you slightly less intelligent with every page you attempt to read • More promise than payoff . . . doesn't make it a bad read • Not as good as her usual writing

6. **A review-writing formula.** Again, how closely you follow a set formula for writing a review depends on the type of review, objectives, length, and how much time you want to take to share your feedback. Here is a simple formula:

   • **Context**: Why are you writing the review? Why this book or author? Perhaps you have certain qualifications or you can set it to current events.

   • **Summarize**: Briefly describe the plot, setting, scope; but don't give away key details. Refrain from adding spoilers but if you must, clearly state that in the review so readers can choose to stop reading.

- **Critique**: This is the meat of the review so have opinion and talk about likes and/or dislikes. How does it compare to other books or authors, or your own experience? Giving specific examples is especially good.
- **Objectivity**: Consider sharing something negative or critical.
- **Closing**: Make a recommendation; share final thoughts and comments.

Writing reviews: An interview with Midwest Book Review's Marj Charlier

In this interview with Midwest Book Review's Marj Charlier, we'll go deep into specific details of review writing. Marj has been a staff reporter for the *Wall Street Journal*, owns a small publishing company, and has written eleven novels—both traditionally published and self-published. It's the perfect background and experience for answering questions about a range of topics, such as:

- Her process or formula for writing a review vs. reviews from the *New York Times.*
- Writing fiction reviews vs nonfiction reviews.
- How she reviews self-published books relative to traditionally published books.

- Writing professional vs. reader reviews.

1. Are there required steps to follow when reviewing a book, or points that every review should cover?

Marj: I don't think there are any required steps, but there are some general conventions that have developed in the industry for the kind of reviews that appear in major newspapers in the US, particularly the Sunday *New York Times Book Review*. Not everyone follows these conventions, and there are ways to write about books that aren't reviews.

I describe writing fiction reviews this way:

1. Start with a related, but not on the nose, comment about the world, your life, or the author.
2. Describe the book's place in the world (genre, popularity, other critical acclaim or disclaim).
3. Summarize the plot.
4. Opine on the plot, the prose, and the character development.
5. Say something negative that proves your objectivity.
6. Wrap it up with a final comment on the value (or not) of the book.

The process for a nonfiction book is different only in that it summarizes the main topics of the book, and evaluates their completeness, accuracy, or fairness.

What I try to include in my shorter reviews (usually only about 500 words versus the *NYT's* 1,000) are four things:

1. Some context (either from my life or the author's life).
2. A summary of the book (but never a spoiler that gives away the solution to the mystery or the secret the author is keeping until the end).
3. A critique of the element I found most striking or intriguing, whether it's the plot, the characters, or the prose. The critique can be positive or negative.
4. I like to end with a recommendation, simply up or down.

This is doable in 500 words, which is about as much as the Midwest Book Review accepts.

5. **What is your process for reviewing a book?**
Marj: I generally read the book all the way through without taking notes in order to reproduce a typical reader's approach. I let my thoughts about it ferment in my head for about a week, until I sense what lasting impact it has had on me, decide what my main conclusion will be, and then sit down to write. I generally

have the book with me, so I can fact-check myself when it comes to names or plot points. I let the review sit in my computer for a couple of days so I can edit or rewrite as necessary, which is only possible after getting that separation.

I read about a book a week, and review about half of them. I put all my reviews on my website and send a couple every month to *Midwest Book Review.*

6. **Does your review process change when reviewing self-published books?**

    Marj: The process doesn't change, but I will generally tread a bit lighter on the critique of self-published books. I know how difficult it is to get a self-published book in readers' hands, and I don't want to be part of the problem. For the same reason, I don't review self-published books that I wouldn't recommend.

    If I think it's poorly written or poorly plotted—whatever—and I think the negatives outweigh the positives, I just decline to review it. That brings me into frequent conflict with my writer friends, some of whom I've upset by never "getting around" to reviewing their books on Amazon.

7. **What is the difference between writing a "professional review" vs. a "reader review,"**

or are there any? If you write both, how do you approach the process?

Marj: I write both, although I write far more "professional" reviews than consumer reviews. Because I usually review traditionally published books, I feel that adding my consumer review to the 1,420 already posted on Amazon is a waste of time.

The difference, largely, is breadth and depth. As a consumer of both "reader" reviews (read: Amazon and Goodreads) and professional book reviews, I expect different things from them.

Like most Amazon customers, I want to know what the book is about and whether the reader liked it or not, and why. That can be accomplished in two sentences or in ten. Anything longer is too long.

Most readers aren't as interested in deep critiques of a writer's prose or an analysis of the writer's development as an artist.

On the other hand, I am frustrated by many reader reviews—the ones full of grammatical errors, spelling mistakes, or failures of logic. Whether positive or negative, these weaknesses make me distrust the review's writer. I am also frustrated when a consumer-reviewer "likes" or "hates" a book but isn't able to tell me why. (I might like a book for the same reason someone else hated it.)

I find it unfair and a waste of my time when a consumer gives a book a one-star review because they don't like the politics or religion of the author. And finally, it bothers me when readers review the book they wanted to read, not the one they read. "I wish she would have written about . . ." or "This should have been a story about . . ." are examples of comments that aren't helpful.

I once received a spate of one-star, no-comment reviews from friends of a woman who was going through a divorce with a golfing buddy of mine. Another time, a reader gave one of my books one star because one of my major characters was overweight, which she found "insensitive." That's all she said about the book. ·

How helpful is that? These kinds of reviews delegitimize consumer reviews on Amazon and Goodreads for everyone.

Learn by reading popular reviews

I want to end this topic of how to write reviews by suggesting that you read some reader-favorite reviews for inspiration and to see what works for people who use reviews to inform their buying decision. Many of us are familiar with Amazon's most "helpful" reviews. The number of helpful votes is shown below the review. Their system will also pull out the top positive review and the top critical review.

Perhaps an even better source of examples is the list of reviews featured in the annual "most read book reviews" published by *Publishers Weekly*. They say that they review more than 8,000 books each year and these are the most read. Here are the two most recent lists:

The Most-Read Book Reviews of 2018:
http://breve.link/brc24

The Most-Read Book Reviews of 2017:
http://breve.link/brc25

Publishing your book review

Sources 4 through 9 listed in Chapter 4 need people to write reviews. They have guidelines and an application process that you need to be familiar with or qualify for before your review is published. I link below to several to give you an idea of what is involved.

But let's say you are writing a review for one of the other four reasons noted at the outset (expert status, content, free books, meeting people). In this case you need to think like a book blogger.

A book blogger writes their review and publishes it in many places, not just their blog. It doesn't have to be an exact copy in each place, but why take all that time to write a review and then not place it in as many places as possible? It is called repurposing content and it's smart.

TIP: Always be mindful of copyright laws. If you write and submit a review for publication (paid or unpaid), understand your ownership of that review and what you can and cannot do with it.

By the same token, others—such as the author of the book you reviewed—must respect your copyright for the review you wrote. They can generally use excerpts but not the entire review without your permission.

My advice is to be proactive about this by encouraging the author to use excerpts you select or require them to seek your approval. All quotes should be attributed, and attributed in a manner that meets your approval. Remember, this is essentially marketing for you—much like a blurb, as noted in Chapter 6.

Marketing your review

After publishing the *The Book Reviewer Yellow Pages*, I reached out to everyone who reviewed earlier editions to see if they would review this latest one. (See what I did there? Always contact reviewers that liked your previous work.) One reviewer in particular made an impression on me.

After posting the review, she asked me to share her review on social media and to vote it "helpful" on Amazon. Her goal was to move up the ranks of reviewers and this is only possible if people read and voted for her reviews. It was a reminder that there is more to "writing a review" than simply posting it or sending it off. When appropriate, you should also market it.

Become a reviewer: examples of businesses looking for review writers

These are just a handful of links to places that you can apply to be a reviewer. I list them here only to stimulate your thinking by taking you directly to their application page. For more, simply return to Chapter 4 and explore the business listed in sources 4 to 8, and several in source 9.

1. Kirkus: http://breve.link/brc26
2. Reedsy: http://breve.link/brc27
3. San Francisco Book Review: http://breve.link/brc28
4. Midwest Book Review (includes advice about writing reviews): http://breve.link/brc29
5. American Book Review's FAQ number four, found here: http://breve.link/brc30

10

Putting It All Together

"Reviews can impact discoverability,
search ranking, and customer trust. A
product's first review has been shown to
increase sales by up to 3.5x."
— Amazon.com, Inc.

Few new authors are truly prepared for the task of book marketing following the release of their book. You successfully navigate the challenges of writing, editing, production, and distribution only to discover yet another mountain to climb—marketing.

If there is one thing I've learned after publishing more than one hundred books on behalf of authors across all genres, it is that there is a gray zone between "produce the book" and "market the book." It is not a black-and-white cut-off. What you do during the latter stages of publishing your book has enormous impact on your ability to sell it.

In *The Book Review Companion* I've concentrated on a core requirement for making any book successful: the task of proactively seeking book reviews. But as we've discovered, this task touches on and is influenced by many other factors, such as time, attitude, networking, and strategy.

We've covered a wide range of sources and some strategies, so rather than summarize those here I am sharing seven core principals. Every time you come across an opportunity to market your book, or as you are evaluating where to spend your time and money, come back to these seven points for guidance.

1. Give yourself a two- to three-month runway and don't rush your book to market. The time spent before release date is worth far more than the first thirty to sixty days after launch. This is especially true for new authors who are still learning about book marketing, not to mention the process of publishing a book.

2. Get book reviews before promoting your book beyond your immediate network. When you finally do get those strangers to your page on Amazon, you want "social proof" in place to alleviate any anxiety about whether they should buy your book.

3. Go out of your way to market your book to your ideal reader. You will have fewer disappointed readers (and poor reviews) and that can lead to better sales. This also helps Amazon market your book to buyers of similar books (see Chapter 8, number six; the discussion about Also Boughts). Who we *can* market to is not always the same group that we *should* market to. If you do not have a way to reach these potential readers, you will need to create it.

4. Start, build, and maintain a mailing list. Even if you plan to write one book, you still need a way to inform those who know you that you have a book coming out. This is the difference between a successful second and third book author, and a one-release dud.

5. Remain focused on getting reviews, and using the reviews you do get well after the release date. Encourage readers to leave reviews, actively seek feedback, and mine those reviews for insights and phrases you can use in marketing, or to improve your writing.

6. Look for ways to thank those who help you, and opportunities to build your network. Use your own platform—your social media network, your website, your mailing list—to publicly acknowledge others, even those who might not be directly related to your book or immediate goals. Your community will notice.

7. Amazon is not the only place people learn about books. Be curious about how people found out about you and your book. Explore these other communities as possible sources of additional reviewers.

• • • • •

Wait. There's more! Your book review journey doesn't stop here. I have two additional bonus sections for you to check out. One is a check list of things you need before you reach out to reviewers. The second is written specifically for new authors.

And finally, I've created a special guide you can share with your prospective reviewers. It is a customizable template that makes it super-simple for your reviewers to leave a review for your book by clicking a single link. Get it here: http://breve.link/brc31

Two Final Things

Would you mind leaving a few words about this book in a review on Amazon, Goodreads, or wherever you bought it? It doesn't have to be long or detailed—the main purpose is to share your opinion. This helps other readers decide if my book might be valuable to them.

Thanks, I really appreciate it.

Once again, each time I release a book or training resource I offer everyone on my mailing list advance notice about an exclusive launch offer. If you'd like to get notified, please visit DavidWogahn.com/join to sign-up or subscribe to one of the free resources at AuthorImprints.com.

You'll be a member of my low-volume mailing list and can unsubscribe anytime. Readers enjoy insightful interviews and high-value articles about book marketing and publishing.

Visit **DavidWogahn.com/join.**

PS. Don't forget to grab my free "leave a review with one click" guide. Customize the template and share it with everyone that reads your book: http://breve.link/brc31

Also by David Wogahn

Learn more at
DavidWogahn.com/mpi

Learn more at
DavidWogahn.com/ryb

Learn more at
DavidWogahn.com/bryp

Bonus 1

Reviewer Outreach Checklist

———

Before you begin contacting any reviewers, it pays to spend time getting organized. It will save you time in the long run, and help you avoid missing opportunities or making mistakes— like contacting the same person twice, using the wrong reviewer's name, or not following up properly.

Follow the guidance below to setup your record-keeping system.

Create a log to track your outreach

Keep track of contact date, website name, URL, contact name, and how you contacted them (email address if email, or note if you used their form). Include a notes field and keep it up to date. A next follow-up date is good too.

Use whatever tool you feel comfortable using and above all—keep good notes. Use a spreadsheet or just a table in Word. Both Microsoft and Google have free online versions. Old-fashioned paper and pen are fine, too.

Stay organized.

Assemble materials

Keep in mind that you are not going to send every-thing noted below to every blogger or reviewer you contact. Send them only what they ask for, and only once you have permission to send it.

The easiest thing to do is have all of the following information in a single document to make it easy to copy/paste where needed. Much of this is also useful if you are the one responsible for setting up distribution of your book. This ensures consistency.

1. Basic metadata (the information that describes your book).
   a. Title and subtitle
   b. Author name or pen name (the way you want it presented publicly)
   c. Publisher or imprint name (if none, state self-published)
   d. ISBN (or ISBNs, if you have a print book and an eBook)
   e. Release date
   f. Number of pages
   g. Word count
   h. Your book description (edited!)
2. Book categories

3. The names of all the books in a series (if applicable).

4. The formats your book is available to read—paperback, hardcover, PDF, Mobi, EPUB, MP3, etc.

5. One or more blurbs, if you have them.

6. If your book is already for sale, collect all those links so you can quickly copy/paste.

7. Links to online reviews of your book, if you have any.

8. Book covers. Besides a large image (1000 pixels on the smallest side), keep a few others on hand such as 150, 300, and 500 pixels wide. Use a free graphics program such as https://pixlr.com/ to size your cover as needed.

9. Links to all your online profiles, as well as current stats (e.g., followers and connections): Goodreads, Facebook, Twitter, LinkedIn, your website, AuthorCentral profile, etc.

TIP: The online currency for many bloggers—how they measure success—are things like social media followers, website traffic, and the size of their mailing list. These bloggers love authors who can help them increase those numbers. An author with the ability to promote the blogger's review may have an easier time getting a book blogger to accept their book than the author who has no such ability.

Bonus 2

The New Author Conundrum: Getting Book Reviews

We can cut to the chase: There is no magic answer. Reviews for any book—from a new author or one who has published a hundred books—traditionally published or self-published, come from three sources:

1. Contacts: people the author can contact.
2. Money: from the author's marketing budget.
3. Sales: as in sales of their book, be it free or paid sales.

Let's take each one of these and look at the options for the new author. This advice is most applicable for books within sixty days of their release.

1. Contacts

I always have my eye out for advice to authors about getting book reviews. Invariably the advice is "Ask your fans!" Or as one I recently came across said, you need to have a strong team behind you. He then went on to describe his beta readers. Other authors talk about their street team. But what if this is your first book, and maybe your only book? Chances are you don't have any "teams" or previous readers to rely on. Even if you are willing to give your book away, who do you give it to?

So how does the new author achieve this?

- By telling everyone they know about their new book
- Connecting with readers who like similar books
- Creating a mailing list

Therefore, it is important to begin building and tracking relationships early and before you release your book. It's why authors with mailing lists, and to a lesser extent a social media following, get more reviews (and sell more books). I call this an Addressable Audience—people you can contact directly.

Your ability to accumulate reviews quickly, in the first thirty days of release, is directly related to the size of your network. This pays off for you in two ways:

1. Your network is most likely to leave the first reviews a book gets.
2. These reviews are more likely to be positive reviews. Why? Those who know you and don't like your book will be less inclined to leave any review, especially a negative review.

There is no shortage of helpful advice about building a social media following, if that's your cup of tea. Personally, I prefer focusing on a mailing list of email addresses. Research has repeatedly shown that members of mailing lists are far more engaged than social media followers.

TIP: Don't hesitate to remind your contacts about their commitment to review your book or to buy it and leave a review. But at some point you need to back off or risk damaging a relationship. Perhaps they simply didn't like your book. Fine, move on.

Ideas for starting and building an email list

There are all sorts of courses, books, and articles available on this topic. I'll share a few ideas to get you started. Note that the advice here is intended to stimulate ideas and not serve as a how-to guide.

- Collect the name and email address of everyone you know.

- Tell them about your book at least a month before its release date. (Use an email service such as MailChimp, Constant Contact, or similar.)
- Keep adding names to the list. Do this manually or automate it by connecting your email service to your website so people can add themselves to your list.
- Ask your mailing list if they want an ARC. If your list is large, set limits.
- Don't be concerned if all you have at the beginning is a list of friends, family, clients, or customers. You can always ask them to share your offer with their friends. (Obviously use your judgment about encouraging immediate family to write reviews.)
- Remember, you are trying to get book reviews at this stage, not sell books.

If this sounds like a lot of work, it is. I also hear a few groans from authors wondering, "Wait, if I'm only seeking reviews from my contacts, when or how am I going to sell books?"

The majority of people reading this do not have an email list or certainly a large mailing list. In my experience, it is better for authors in this situation to use their list to solicit book reviews than to sell books. For those that do have larger lists, those lists can surely be segmented such that you solicit reviews from a subset of your list—those most willing and able to help you—and ask the remaining list members to buy it.

 There are lots of resources for setting up a mailing list but I have created one specifically for new authors. It's called Getting Started Using Email Marketing and you can find it here: http://breve.link/brc7.

2. Money

I consider reviews part of book marketing and as such they are something to budget for. In fact, for those with financial resources this can be a good investment.

Recall the two primary benefits of asking your contacts to review your book.

1. Contacts who know you are more likely to leave the early reviews.
2. Contacts who know you are more likely to leave positive reviews.

With that in mind, here are a few ways to spend your budget.

- Buy copies of your book for reviewers.
- Give prospective reviewers gift certificates.
- Hire someone to research and contact potential reviewers.

- Pay a service like Hidden Gems, NetGalley, or Goodreads to offer your book to their mailing list.
- Hire a blog tour service to conduct a review tour. (See Chapter 4.)
- Pay a service to advertise your book (more on this below).

A few months ago, I was contacted by a small publisher on behalf of their author Dan Janal. She found my review of Ryan Holiday's *Perennial Seller* and decided I would be a good fit to review Dan's book. I agreed and she mailed me a free copy. (It's a good book and I wrote a glowing review.)

Someone had to pay her to research and contact potential reviewers. They also had to pay for the book and postage. My point is that paying someone to do this is a worthwhile investment for any author who can afford it.

Did the author lose a sale? Probably not since I wouldn't have heard of the book otherwise. That's what leads us to the third way to get book reviews.

3. Sales

It's axiomatic; if no one is reading your book, how can you get any reviews? The obvious solution is to get your book into the hands of readers. If you have few contacts, and aren't willing or able to invest money, the next best thing is to give your book away or at least put it on sale.

If you believe you can simply list a book with no or few reviews on Amazon at a price comparable to competing books, and expect readers to gobble it up, you are mistaken. Listing a book for sale on any website is not marketing.

This point was driven home for me after I started using Amazon Advertising (formerly AMS) to promote *Register Your Book*. After two years the reviews had stopped coming in and the book was stuck with twenty-two. After about eight months of advertising it had thirty-two reviews. (I also make more money now since every dollar I spend on advertising returns about $3 in royalties.)

Selling books is clearly everyone's goal. But at the early stages of its release, when getting reviews is most important, there are only two ways to increase "sales" for the purpose of getting reviews:

1. Give your eBook away for free. Join KDP Select and give your book away for up to five days.
2. Run a promotion at a low price, preferably ninety-nine cents.

Keep in mind that using free or cheap eBooks to get reviews is not as effective as it was a few years ago. But if you have few contacts and no or little money, it's your best option. Otherwise you are relying on prayer and luck.

Recapping: the order of these three options—contacts, money, sales—is intentional. They follow the Book Reviewer Journey illustrated in Chapter 2.

1. Your **contacts** are the easiest to leverage and will yield the highest-rated reviews.
2. Spending **money** to target reviewers is the next best option. You at least have some level of control over whom to approach.
3. Getting the book into reader's hands via **sales** is the third option. If discounts and promotions are all you can do, it's better than nothing.

 For those less comfortable using technology, hiring an experienced author assistant is a must. Most book marketing today, especially for self-published books, is online. You can use this individual to help set up and maintain a mailing list, organize promotions, create Amazon Ads, and do the necessary outreach.

About the Author

David Wogahn is a LinkedIn Learning author and the author of five books including *My Publishing Imprint* and *The Book Reviewer Yellow Pages*.

The content of his books draws from his in-depth experience as president of the award-winning author-services company AuthorImprints.com. AuthorImprints.com has helped more than 125 authors professionally self-publish books using their own publishing imprint.

During David's 30 years in publishing and online media, he has worked for the *Los Angeles Times*, the Los Angeles Olympic Organizing Committee, and was co-founder of the first online publisher of sports team branded websites known today as the CBS College Sports Network.

He is a frequent speaker and trainer, including presentations for the Independent Book Publishers Association, the Alliance of Independent Authors (ALLi), the Independent Writers of Southern California, and the Santa Barbara Writers Conference.

Contact David by visiting DavidWogahn.com or AuthorImprints.com.